ROCKY MOUNTAIN

FRUIT & VEGETABLE GARDENING

*Plant, Grow, and Harvest
the Best Edibles*

Quarto is the authority on a wide range of topics.

Quarto educates, entertains and enriches the lives of our readers—enthusiasts and lovers of hands-on living.

www.quartoknows.com

First published in 2014 by Cool Springs Press, an imprint of Quarto Publishing Group USA Inc., 400 First Avenue North, Suite 400, Minneapolis, MN 55401 USA. Telephone: (612) 344-8100. Fax: (612) 344-8692

quartoknows.com
Visit our blogs at quartoknows.com

Cool Springs Press titles are also available at discounts in bulk quantity for industrial or sales-promotional use. For details write to Special Sales Manager at Cool Springs Press, 400 First Avenue North, Suite 400, Minneapolis, MN 55401, USA.

Library of Congress Cataloging-in-Publication Data

Maranhao, Diana.
   Rocky Mountain fruit & vegetable gardening : plant, grow, and harvest the best edibles / Diana Maranhao.
      pages cm
   Other title: Rocky Mountain fruit and vegetable gardening
   Includes index.
   ISBN-13: 978-1-59186-613-8
   ISBN 978-1-59186-613-8 (sc)
   1. Fruit—Rocky Mountains. 2. Nuts—Rocky Mountains. 3. Vegetables—Rocky Mountains. 4.Herbs—Rocky Mountains. 5 Rocky Mountains Region. I. Title. II. Title: Rocky Mountain fruit and vegetable gardening.

   SB355.5.R63M37 2014
   635.0978—dc23

                              2013050315

Acquisitions Editor: Mark Johanson
Design Manager: Cindy Samargia Laun
Horticultural Editor: Troy Marden
Layout: S. E. Anderson

Printed in China

10 9 8 7 6 5 4 3 2

ROCKY MOUNTAIN

FRUIT & VEGETABLE GARDENING

Plant, Grow, and Harvest
the Best Edibles

DIANA MARANHAO

COOL SPRINGS PRESS
Home and Garden Experts™

MINNEAPOLIS, MINNESOTA

CONTENTS

PART II

PREFACE

When I was asked to work on a book that had to do with what I do every day of the year, I jumped into the project enthusiastically. I garden every day. Some days, I toil the entire day to plant and sow the season's crops. And some days, I garden just a few minutes when I trudge through the snow out to the greenhouse to make sure everything made it through the single digit winter night. I may only put my finger in the soil of the potted herbs to see if they are thirsty or pluck a leaf from the aromatic and delicious bay laurel, but these are the gardening tasks that keep me grounded during the long winter season and keep me dreaming of harvests to come.

I gardened in the Pacific Northwest as a child but never really took to the task. I loved eating the fruits of our labors but didn't see the sense in running out to dig in the just thawed, cold soil in a frenzy to get the corn in so it would grow and produce before first frost. I thought the whole business a dirty and much too laborious affair when I should be playing. It wasn't until I found myself living on a couple of acres in a rural area of southern California, with two small children to feed on a limited budget, that I took

Your fruit or vegetable garden doesn't need to be this big in order for you to enjoy fresh produce!

up a shovel and commenced to garden. I didn't know anything about what I was trying to do, but I was determined to put some food on the table.

Fortunately I was gardening in a lovely fenced-in plot that had been dug, turned, and planted for years by an elderly lady that grew her own food there for many seasons. She hauled sand up from the creek bed, burned her trash in the garden incinerator then spread the ashes, buried her kitchen scraps directly in the beds to turn to compost, and broke up glass bottles in an old burlap sacknand buried those too, serving as gopher deterrents. Although she had passed many years before, her gardening lessons lived on in the rich luscious soil she left me that yielded bountiful harvests for my family. It was these successes that led me to a long career in horticulture and that continue to fuel the passion I have for gardening to this day.

There is a fever in the air. From a country that has its beginnings in farming, evolving to the high-tech world we live in today, we are going back to our roots. The economy had something to do with it, but living a healthy life and providing the family with fresh fruits and vegetables fed the fever. From condominium dwellers and their patio gardens and homeowners replacing their lawns with edible landscapes to a migration back to the country and to the land to build small organic farms, more and more novice and seasoned gardeners want to grow at least a part of their own produce, and for those that are not inclined, to seek out the farmers that are growing and selling their harvests at the farmer's markets.

As I look over past garden journal entries, the challenges differ from year to year, season to season. I have had some failures, but more successes, and it's the successes that keep farmers farming and keep gardeners gardening. I intend to fill your head with success stories, to share the lessons I have learned, and to feed the gardening fever. There is nothing more gratifying than to step out your front door, pluck a tomato from the vine, wipe it off on your shirt and just bite in. With gardeners, it is as much about the journey as it is about the destination.

My goal is to take the mystery out of gardening, to make it easy to garden and to encourage everyone to garden who wants to. For new gardeners, the task is daunting. Where to start? How to plan? Where to buy the plants? How to plant them? What if there is a disease that wipes everything out? How do I know when to pick or to harvest? What do I do with it once I have it? This book will address those questions, but in a clear and honest way to make your journey smooth. The important thing is that you begin, pick up a hand trowel, a shovel, a pot, a bag of soil, a packet of seed. All you need to add is water. Really! It's that simple.

—Diana

PART I

GROWING EDIBLES IN THE ROCKY MOUNTAIN STATES

A garden is an ever-changing thing. Novices just starting down the gardening path are faced with an endless list of details to pay attention to, new terminology and concepts to absorb, decisions of what to grow and where to grow it, maintaining the garden, and then, what to do with it when it actually produces fruit or vegetables. Seasoned gardeners know that although they may follow the same basic gardening steps and use the best garden practices honed over years of experience, every season is different. Some years, the magic works, and some years, crops fall short of the goal. Too many variables to note, except in our garden journals, we continue to garden year after year, season after season. Once you have planted your first seed and bit into your first home grown tomato, you will be hooked and soon take your place among the seasoned gardeners.

Scarlet runner beans growing up trellises are as pretty as they are tasty!

This book is meant for all gardeners. It is small enough in size to throw it in your shopping bag when you venture to the local garden center and need help selecting edibles that grow easily in our Rocky Mountain region, in deciding whether to buy seed or starts, what sorts of fruit trees to look for, types of irrigation available, and the difference between mulch and compost. Carry it to the office, where it will guide you through the garden planning process, from scheduling your crops to designing a garden space to be the perfect home for your plants. Put it in the garden trug, where it begins with working with the soil, soil testing and recommendations, preparing the soil for planting, sowing seed, and planting bare-root and container plants. There are charts for determining how many frost-free days you have to grow, how much cold plants can take, and diagrams for how to plant trees. Learn what weeds are and how to keep the garden healthy and thriving. And finally, within the plant profiles, learn when and how to bring in the bountiful harvest.

The variables may change. Mother Nature leaves her distinct mark on everything that happens in the garden. With *Rocky Mountain Fruit & Vegetable Gardening* by your side, you will be able to deal with whatever comes your way. The important thing is that you grow (garden) and continue growing (gardening)!

The Rocky Mountain range covers a vast amount of land, including the five states that it passes through: Idaho, Montana, Wyoming, Colorado, and Utah. The mountains run north and south, following a diagonal line encompassing over half of Colorado, just touching the southern corner of Utah, passing through the western regions of Wyoming and Montana and filling the panhandle of Idaho. The mountains reach their greatest height in Colorado at Mount Elbert at 14,400 feet, in sheer contrast to expanses of desert shared by each of the five states. Desert regions range from low desert, low rainfall, arid environments to high desert elevations of 4,800 feet that usually experience snowfall in winter.

Within the five Rocky Mountain states, there are no less than three USDA Zone ranges in each state. Utah, with extreme elevation and topography changes, hosts USDA Zones 4 through 8, with low temperature ranges from a balmy 10°F in the low desert to 30°F below 0 in the upper mountain regions in the northern most parts of the state. Montana, with half of the state being within the Rocky Mountain range, falls within USDA Zones 3 and 4, with temperatures frequently falling from minus 20°F to minus 30°F.

We use USDA Zonal maps as a guide for determining which trees, shrubs, and perennials are hardy enough to grow in our zones at the extreme coldest temperatures. If you find your area on a boundary line between zones, always use the lowest temperature range zone as your guide. This will assure the ability of the plants to survive in those temperature extremes and go a long way in assuring success of your edibles. Information noting plant cold hardiness is readily available in plant reference guides and on plant labels.

Fruits, nut trees, and berries are long-lived edibles and march to their own list of needs. They have chill requirements, the number of hours that temperatures need to be below 45°F for fruit to set. Required chill hours are usually designated within a range, but the minimum chill hours number must be met in order to have fruit. Breeders are constantly working on low-chill varieties, which will have lower requirements than those stated. The Cooperative Extension, local fruit growers, and garden centers will be able to give you lists of specific varieties that grow best in your locality. More on chill hours in Chapter 7.

USDA Plant Hardiness Zone Maps

Colorado, Idaho, Montana, Utah, and Wyoming

The United States Department of Agriculture (USDA) has developed hardiness zone ranges for all of North America. Hardiness refers to the ability of a plant to continue to grow at the corresponding lowest temperatures for the particular zone. For example, garden sage is listed as surviving to USDA Zone 2. This means that if temperatures fall to 40 or even 50 degrees below 0, the plant will survive. Some plants can withstand a few nights of cold temps falling below their zonal range, but this is dependent upon a number of other conditions such as soil moisture, plant health, protection from the elements, and other environmental factors. This chart is a listing of average minimum temperatures and zones and should only be used as a guide to selecting plants that are rated as zone appropriate for your region.

Carrots are easy to grow in the Rocky Mountains.

Colorado

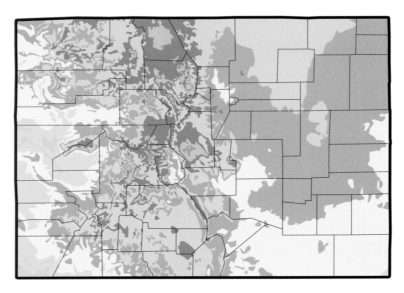

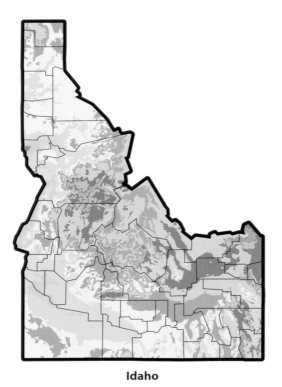

Idaho

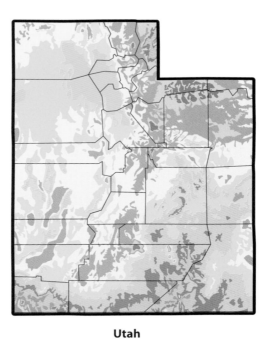

Utah

Montana

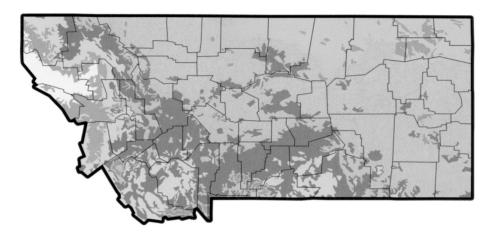

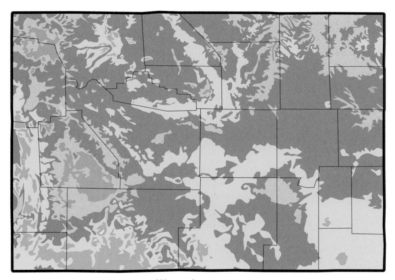

Wyoming

ZONE	Average Minimum Temperature		ZONE		
2A	-45 to -50		7A	5 to 0
2B	-40 to -45		7B	10 to 5
3A	-35 to -40		8A	15 to 10
3B	-30 to -35		8B	20 to 15
4A	-25 to -30		9A	25 to 20
4B	-20 to -25		9B	30 to 25
5A	-15 to -20		10A	35 to 30
5B	-10 to -15		10B	40 to 35
6A	-5 to -10		11	40 and Above
6B	0 to -5			

CHAPTER 1

THE ROCKY MOUNTAIN REGION

Gardeners in the Rocky Mountain regions experience different growing conditions depending on where they live. Covering five states (Colorado, Idaho, Montana, Utah, and Wyoming) this book details growing information for a large area. Northernmost sections experience extreme winter cold, a late spring, and a short summer. Southern areas experience hot summers and low humidity. Soil types, rain and snowfall, summer heat (or lack thereof), and geographical features all influence plant growth, and what you plant, and when you plant it is highly influenced by the growing conditions where you live.

To be sure, gardening in such a varied geographical region has its challenges, starting with the ground up. Rocky Mountain soils are alkaline in nature and range from clayey to sandy, depending upon a number of geological and climatic factors.

Fortunately, in the business of growing most annual edibles, the 7.0 to 8.3 pH range really doesn't come into play, as they are not directly affected by slightly alkaline soils. The degree of alkalinity may have some affect on the availability of nutrients to the plants, but these deficiencies are easy enough to deal with when the plants show you what they lack.

Water conservation and gardening in drought conditions are common threads among Rocky Mountain gardeners that unite us in efforts to make the most out of the water we have and to conserve our use, both inside and outside of the home. Growing edibles takes water, but there are many ways to eliminate waste and to direct the flow. Drip or micro-irrigation systems, careful scheduling of watering cycles, companion planting, and use of mulches are the tools of trade. The crops will be healthier for your water conserving efforts, and healthy plants are better able to thwart off pests and disease.

For the most part, timing annual vegetable and fruit crops is key. Some cool-season annuals may be planted before the last frost, but many will still need to be sowed indoors in winter or purchased as starts in order to get them producing by the time either summer heat (if early spring planted) or winter freezes are a regular event (if late summer sowed). Warm season annuals need a specific number of frost-free days to grow and to produce, so getting them in the ground, either as plant starts or by sowing seed, must occur at the earliest and safest time in spring.

Last season frosts may come in the early spring in valley and desert elevations, catching fruit trees in bloom. Planting late blooming and early fruiting cultivars helps with the timing, planting on hills and mounds keeps frost-sensitive flowers out of frost pockets, and by providing crop cover, air circulation, and some bit of warmth, we can bring fruit trees to their harvest.

First frosts come at a time when the winter squash stems are still toughening up or the tomatoes on the vine continue to ripen with each day of sunshine. Some crops may be harvested early and hung in the greenhouse or set on a warm windowsill to finish ripening. Others just need a little more time, so it is worth the effort to pull a layer of crop cover over top

GROWING TIP

Plant choices for cooler areas can be limited by the number of frost-free days in the growing season. When selecting seeds for pumpkins and melons—two plants that take a long time to grow from seed to flower to fruit—check to make sure you have enough frost-free days to grow them and start them early and transplant seedlings to jumpstart the crop.

when first frost threatens. The date may change from year to year, so always be on the safe side and be patient with Mother Nature. You will soon fall into her rhythm in subsequent seasons.

Higher elevations of the Rocky Mountain regions face a very small window of growing opportunity with first frost dates appearing early in the growing season, as soon as 50 days after the last frost. Summers are cooler, which cool-season crops love, but growing warm-season crops can be a challenge in these areas. Selecting plants that need the least number of days from seed to harvest makes the growing schedule more attainable. Extending the season, either by starting seeds early indoors or in a greenhouse or cold frame gives plants a jumpstart on the season.

Warm-season crops, like tomatoes, need 70 to 80 days to grow and produce (depending upon the type), if planted from a transplant, and 120 days from seed to harvest. Tomatoes need four to six weeks to germinate and to get to transplant size. If you are growing your own seedlings, then you would count backwards six to eight weeks (allows a couple of weeks to harden off) from the last frost date to determine when to start the heat mat to sow the seed indoors. If you rely on the local nursery to grow your starts for you, then you can figure planting just after the last projected frost date. Then count forward 80 days from planting to determine how much protection, if any, you will need to provide to get the crop to harvest.

Use the frost table as a jumping off point to calculate and schedule your crops and growing season tasks. Frost dates will deviate depending upon your specific location and elevation. For example, in low desert elevations, the last frost may occur in early April, so most folks will have their gardens planted by mid-month. However, just 25 miles southeast, the elevation climbs another 2,000 feet to the high desert region at 4,800 feet, where the last frost isn't until April 30, making planting safe after the first week in May.

Average Projected Last and First Frost Dates

City	Last Frost	First Frost	Average Frost-Free Days
COLORADO			
Denver	5/4	10/2	151
Durango	7/3	8/27	55
Ft. Collins	5/4	10/2	152
La Junta	5/1	10/2	154
Steamboat Springs	6/27	8/30	64
IDAHO			
Boise	5/6	10/8	155
Idaho Falls	6/17	9/3	78
Moscow	5/12	9/27	138
Salmon	5/7	10/25	131
Sandpoint	5/26	9/14	111
MONTANA			
Billings	5/4	10/1	150
Bozeman	6/4	9/12	100
Glendive	5/22	9/11	112
Helena	7/3	8/18	46
Libby	5/25	9/20	118
UTAH			
Cedar City	5/21	10/1	133
Joseph	5/16	10/5	142
Mexican Hat	4/18	10/22	187
Salt Lake City	5/1	10/12	164
St. George	4/26	10/24	181
WYOMING			
Casper	5/16	9/13	120
Cheyenne	5/12	9/26	134
Jackson	7/10	8/16	37
Laramie	6/15	9/11	88
Powell	5/19	9/18	122

*Check with your local Cooperative Extension agent for annual projected dates.
Dates listed here are to be viewed as when the risk of frost may occur. These dates can vary within two weeks either way.

CHAPTER 2

SEASONAL GARDENING

Most annual edible plants that we grow fall into two categories: cool-season plants (that grow best when temperatures are cool—usually below 70°F) and warm-season plants (that grow best when temperatures are warmer—usually above 65°F). For novice gardeners, the distinction between seasonal crops serves as a guideline for knowing which plants prefer cool or warm temperatures to grow well. Seasoned gardeners use warm and cool season plant preferences, specific regional climate patterns, and past gardening experiences to help them make crop scheduling decisions.

In the Rocky Mountain regions, Utah and Idaho have a longer frost-free growing period, with more distinct cool and warm growing seasons. Cool spring temperatures often stick around only a short amount of time, with hot summer temps heating up the soil and the air seemingly overnight. Warm-season crops have an easier go of it in these states. Colder winter climates are prevalent in Colorado, Montana, and Wyoming, and they have a more compressed growing season. Cooler spring and summer temps are perfect for growing cool-season crops.

Heat is a big consideration when growing cool-season crops when the heat of the summer sun signals the plants to end their journey. They will flower or simply curl up and die if the air and soil heats up beyond their comfort zone. Broccoli, beets, Brussels sprouts, lettuce, and spinach either set flower or turn bitter when air and soil temperatures get too hot. Even warm-season crops that

BIENNIAL VEGETABLES

Some plants defy neat categorizing—they grow equally well in warm weather and cold weather. These plants are considered to be biennial. They won't flower and set seed until their second year. Swiss chard and arugula are the two main traditional "cool weather" vegetables that will grow just fine throughout summer if they are planted in spring. Kale will grow throughout summer, as well, though the leaves can be tough and bitter during hotter weather. In colder areas, biennial vegetables are grown as annuals.

Swiss chard is a biennial vegetable.

relish long, warm summers stop growing or abort their fruiting efforts if the heat is turned up too much for an extended period of time. Tomatoes, that normally beginning to flower as the heat of summer sets in, abort their blooms if the daytime temps remain in triple digits for more than a few days.

Soil temperature extremes and fluctuations, either over a few days time or overnight can slow up crops too, but we have gardening methods and materials that can buffer the plants against these elements. I have various garden stakes, pieces of shade cloth and frost protection cloth, and stacks of straw at the ready that I move in and out of the beds and among crops as they need them. Plants are very good at sending out signals when they are displeased (When they are happy, they are producing!), and with experience you will catch their meaning early on to give them some relief to get through temperature tribulations.

Cool-Season and Warm-Season Gardening

In the Rocky Mountain region, cool-season plants thrive from March through May and again in August through October. (Dates vary depending upon where you live.) The warmest season runs from June through September.

Elevation, latitude, climate, and proximity to the Rocky Mountains all contribute to temperature differences between areas within the region. While there are but 11 traveling miles difference between our home and the nearest town, the elevation rises by over 1,000 feet from there to here. Gardens in town are already blooming by the time I am just hardening off the starts to be planted our garden. Salt Lake City gardeners, in the northern part of the state and higher mountain elevations, still have another two to three weeks before they are planting their gardens. Read the labels, know your last frost dates for your area, check the soil temperatures, talk to other gardeners, and read and carry this book! You will be on your way to that first harvest of edibles before you know it!

Bolting

Lettuces, cabbages, broccoli, cauliflower, turnips, and radishes are all cool-season vegetables that will bolt. Dill and cilantro, cool-season herbs, bolt in the heat, but their seeds are as useful in the kitchen as their leaves are, carrying higher oil content. Most cool-season crops bolt in late spring as the days get longer and the temperatures get warmer.

Cool-season herbs and vegetables do not grow well throughout the season in areas that have hot summers. Sometimes it is necessary to provide afternoon shade if summer comes unusually early and you are

Broccoli plants bolting. The part of the broccoli that we eat is the flower. Once the broccoli heads start to grow and bloom, the window of harvest is over.

at the end of the cool-season crop's cycle. My broccoli crop is still setting crowns in mid-June, no matter how mature the plants are when I set them out. In order to get the last of the harvest in and to discourage bolting, I pull a length of shade cloth over the crop to cool the soil and the air down, thus bringing in the final crowns at the end of June when they have fully formed.

Warm-Season Gardening: Turn Up the Heat!

The same goes for trying to grow warm-season vegetables and herbs in cooler weather. Every April, when I go to town, the local nurseries have rack after rack filled with plump tomato, pepper, and squash plants luring me to buy. Realize that they are in the business of selling plants, so they will get the product out in time for the buyer to get a dose of early spring fever. Just because the nursery stocks tomato transplants in April doesn't mean you should plant them outside in April. You can buy them, of course, but take them home, protect them from the still winter-like elements, harden them off, then plant them out after your last frost date.

For those gardeners growing in cooler summer areas, common in high mountain elevations in Rocky Mountain regions, growing warm-season crops is more challenging but possible. Extending the season is key for those wanting to grow their own tomatoes, peppers, summer and winter squash, and other warm-season lovers. Starting the plants early indoors, in a greenhouse or cold frame produces mature, often already setting bloom, healthy plants. Pre-warming the soil only takes a few weeks if you lay out black plastic or weed barrier material to harness the early spring or summer sun's heat. Providing tunnels covered with clear plastic or row cover material protects the crops from late frosts and collects heat into the small area. Container grown crops are confined to pots that heat up the soil and hold the heat longer. To prolong the crop growth into harvest, layers of straw protect the soil from freeze, and crop protection cloth keeps the crops safe from early frosts.

Some Annual Edibles Like It Hot!

These favorite summer vegetables are native to tropical areas and grow only when soil temperatures are warm enough (at least 65°F). Don't plant these outdoors too early, but do start indoors in January, February, or March, depending upon the type. Those marked with an * should be direct sowed/planted outdoors. See individual plant profiles for specifics.

Bean*	Pepper	Sweet potato
Corn*	Potato*	Tomatillo
Cucumber	Pumpkin*	Tomato
Eggplant	Summer squash	Watermelon

Soil Temperature

Buy an inexpensive soil thermometer to help you gauge when to plant different edibles. My soil thermometer lives in the greenhouse during the winter months, where I use it in the seed flats to monitor the temperature of the soil for both cool- (As low as 45°F is preferred.) and warm-season (likes soil temps of at least 65°F) crops. In spring, it gets moved outdoors to various garden beds to make sure the soil is at the temperature the plants need to grow.

Soil thermometer

Diseases are more of a problem in cool, wet soils. Sweet corn seeds will rot in the ground if planted too early when the soil is still cold. Damping off, pythium, and root rot diseases can strike seeds that are planted too early in cool soil. Peppers won't die in a cold soil, but they refuse to grow at all until the soil temperature reaches 70°F. So while it may seem a little thing to do, monitoring the soil temperature plays a big role in making the gardeners life easier, and the plants will thank you for your consideration.

Watering Warm- and Cool-Season Crops

In Rocky Mountain regions we are affected by dwindling water resources, changing weather patterns, periods of long and short droughts, and drying winds coupled with low annual rain and snowfall. Growing your own edibles takes water, but there are many ways to eliminate waste and to direct the flow. Drip or micro-irrigation systems, careful scheduling of watering cycles, companion planting, and use of mulches are the tools of trade. The crops will be healthier for your water conserving efforts and healthy plants are better able to thwart off pests and disease.

Plants send out signals when they are hot, thirsty, or waterlogged. The symptoms are the same, so follow this simple rule:

If a plant wilts, then bend down, use your "pointer" finger, and insert it into the soil. If the soil is dry down to the second joint, then water slowly and deeply. If the soil is moist, then don't water.

When soil temperatures rise, plants often wilt in response. If the soil is damp when you test it, don't water or try to cool the plant down by hosing it off. Watering when it doesn't need it leads to rots and fungal disease. Wetting the leaves accelerates evaporation and dries the leaves out faster, causing scorch. Usually, as evening approaches and the soil and air cools, then the plant regains turgidity. If you are in a prolonged heat spell, grab a piece of shade cloth and a couple of stakes and shade the plants. Be sure the plant is mulched. If water-logging or rots are suspect, then withhold water for long

Corn plants roll up their leaves to prevent water loss.

WHAT'S WRONG WITH MY CORN?

When corn plants don't have enough water available to take up (the soil is too dry), they will roll their leaves up to reduce the amount of surface area exposed, thus lowering the amount of water lost through the leaves. If the corn leaves are rolled up and "pointy," you need to water the plants!

---

enough for the soil to completely dry down to a few inches, then water slowly and deeply. See Chapter 5 for more on watering and irrigation.

Chilling Hours

Some plants not only like, but they also *need* colder air. Most fruit trees need a certain number of hours with air temperatures below 45°F, called chilling hours. Plants with chilling hour requirements must meet the minimum number of chilling hours in order to break dormancy and bloom. (No blooms, no fruits!) During warmer winters, fruit trees can get physiologically "confused," blooming early, late, or not at all. See Chapter 6 for more on chilling hours.

CHAPTER 3

BUILDING GREAT SOIL

The first lesson in growing vegetables and fruits is indeed "rooted" in the soil. The fundamental elements a plant needs to grow—nutrients, moisture, and oxygen are all obtained from it. To build a healthy, productive garden we must start from the ground and work up.

Soil pH

PH is a measurement noting the acidity or alkalinity of soil. This is the first element you will find on a soil test, and it is an important fact to know, because the pH will affect the soil's ability to release the nutrients so that they are available to the plants. It is impossible to alter the chemical pH of soil. Peat, which is acidic, is often incorporated into native alkaline backfill soil at planting time,

A compost bin can keep roots out of your compost and help contain the pile.

giving a good jumpstart to those plants that prefer acidic soil. Eventually the roots of the plant extend far beyond the hole. After just a season or two, the peat will have completely broken down and decomposed, merging with the existing soil. What this means is that we have to work with whatever soil pH we have, rather than try to change it.

Acid (pH range 3.0 to 6.0) soils are typically found in higher elevations in cool, moist, densely vegetated and forested areas. Acid soils are not indigenous to the Rocky Mountain regions, although pockets of mildly acid soils may occur in a few of our higher mountain elevations. Most plants can handle a bit of acidity without much problem.

Rocky Mountain soils share pH ranges from 7.0 to 8.5, so our soils are alkaline in nature. Alkaline soils typically live in places with low rainfall and are high in calcium. Most plants live happily in a slightly alkaline soil. Fruits and vegetables may have to be supplemented with fertilizer if plants show signs of deficiencies during the growing cycle. Typical deficiencies reveal themselves in changes in the leaf color; yellow foliage can be a sign of low nitrogen, yellowing between the veins of the leaf usually signals a lack of iron.

The Perfect Soil

Vegetables and fruits prefer a soil that is rich in nutrients with a medium pH range of 7.0. They relish a compost-laden, fluffy, well draining soil. Most plants like to have their roots in a soil that when water is applied, it percolates gently into the soil profile, filling the air spaces as it goes, finally drifting into the soil beyond the roots of the plant, taking harmful salts with it. The roots send out tiny root hairs to form a deep root network, able to absorb water and nutrients from the soil. The healthy, white roots transport the nutrient-laden water through the vascular system to the growing tips of the plants, plumping up the foliage and encouraging new growth. In a perfect world—a perfect soil—but this is rarely the case.

Soil Texture in the Rocky Mountain Region

Soil texture is a physical property that directly influences all other soil traits. The texture of the soil dictates the amount of air space, how water travels through the soil profile, drainage, and water-holding capabilities. Soil texture plays the most important role in contributing to overall plant health, as water and nutrients must travel through it to the plant roots so it can be absorbed by the plant.

Soil texture refers to the size of the particles in the soil. Sandy soils are made up of large, round soil particles, providing good drainage. Water passes quickly through sandy soils, causing them to dry out faster. Silt is a medium-sized particle. Silt may have been sand at one time, but it is smaller in size, typical of soils in old stream or lake bed areas. It is the most desirable particle as it has great water-holding capabilities, making nutrients available to the plant, but it still drains well. Clay is the smallest of soil particles and more plate-like in shape. It can hold water so tightly that it doesn't release it to the plants—as in waterlogged soils or soils that stay wet for a long time.

A soil test will tell you what the texture of your soil is. Chances are you will have a combination of the three particles, and in all situations the desire is to move the water through the soil to the roots. The best treatment is to incorporate organic matter into the soil on a seasonal basis.

It's important to continually add compost to your raised beds and vegetable gardens.

Add Organic Matter

Organic materials, compost, manures, topsoil mixes, and peat create air spaces in the soil, which means better water movement. The texture of the soil can be altered, but building good textured, well draining soils takes time and patience. Gardeners often ask me how much to add. A simple method is to spread 3 inches of compost over the entire bed, then rototill that in. Do this at the start of each season. If you are compost rich, spread an inch or so on the bed when you close down the garden in winter. It will do some magic over the winter months. It takes at least three seasons of amending with organic matter to start seeing the results of your labors.

How to Compost

If you are short on time, or live in a city, condo, or apartment setting, you will be buying compost. You can get it in a bag or by the truckload, depending upon how big of an area you are planting. If you are container gardening, be sure to buy a light, airy bagged mix formulated for vegetables or fruits. It will have a higher organic content than a potting or propagating soil.

We make our own compost, having started with just a pile and now graduated to four large wooden and wire bins strategically placed at opposite ends of the property. Still, after over six years of composting our kitchen waste (huge quantities during harvest and preserving seasons), pruning debris (from orchard, vineyard, and one acre of ornamental trees) and shrubs, and lawn waste (from two lawns and meadows), we still have to beg or buy more compost. You can never have too much!

Compost Ingredients

There are two types of materials to add to compost piles: green materials, which are high in nitrogen, and brown materials, which are high in carbon. While there isn't a precise ratio of green to brown materials required in compost piles, if you add equal amounts of each over time, you'll get usable compost faster. You can compost almost any natural material, but don't put any animal products other than eggshells in the compost pile. No meat, cheese, or dairy.

Green materials include grass clippings, weeds, green leaves, kitchen scraps, and eggshells. Brown materials include shredded newspapers, dried leaves, sawdust, wood chips, paper bags and towels, twigs, tea bags, wheat straw, and coffee grounds.

Building the Pile

Build a compost pile by layering green materials and brown materials. Start with chopped-up dried leaves (Run over them with the lawn mower.). Then add grass clippings or kitchen scraps, and keep layering. The smaller the pieces you add to the pile, the faster they will decompose. Our biggest investment in the composting operation was the homeowners' chipper/shredder. This saves us labor and decreases the time it makes to make good compost.

Continuously add material to the compost pile—shredded newspapers, the stems of broccoli, last summer's dead annual flowers that you pulled up, even the Halloween pumpkin. Cut up big pieces before putting in the pile. An entire pumpkin, carved face intact, takes a long time to break down. Cut flower stems in half, melons into chunks, vines into pieces to speed the process. From time to time, add a layer of completed compost to the pile.

Keep the pile "cooking" (a healthy pile will heat up) by using a pitchfork or garden fork to turn the pile, mix it up, and oxygenate it. You will need to water it

Compost pile

periodically as well. You don't want sludge, but it needs moisture to decompose and the worms need it to live.

If the compost smells, it is too wet. Add more brown materials to absorb the moisture and turn the pile so that it can dry out. If your pile is not shrinking or decomposing, turn it and water, then add green materials or worms to give it a kick-start. Make sure you cut up materials into smaller pieces before adding.

Other Soil Amendments

There are other types of organic matter that you can add to the soil to provide extra nutrients to plants, either when you're planting or when you're prepping the soil for planting. Follow directions and incorporate soil amendments.

Blood meal, bone meal, and plant tones: organic, slow-release fertilizers made from animal products. Plant tones are available for acid-loving plants, vegetables, flowers, and trees.

Worm castings and soil conditioner: Both are almost entirely composed of humic acid, which is the most decomposed element in soil. Incorporate before planting.

Garden soil and topsoil: Garden soil and topsoil are coarser soils that build up areas of the garden where soil has washed away or for filling raised beds. Thoroughly incorporate native soil and topsoil before planting.

Manure: Cow, rabbit, chicken, and mushroom compost are commonly available in bags. If you get manure from a local farm, make sure that it has been sitting and aging for at least six months. Even then, spread it out, water, and allow it to break down even further. We only apply manures in the fall, allowing them to sit on top of the soil surface through the winter, then rototill in at spring planting time. Ammonia in fresh manure can burn your plants, so always "season" it before using. Never use cat or dog droppings in the garden.

Worm castings

Garden soil

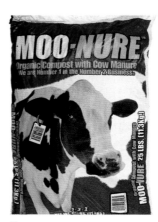

Cow manure

GROWING TIP

You can pick up soil test boxes from your local Cooperative Extension office. Every test result will give you recommendations for adding nitrogen, phosphorus, or potassium. Collect a soil sample to submit by digging clumps of soil from different areas of the garden, mixing them together, and submitting the sample for testing.

Test the Soil

After you've added compost, manure, or topsoil to create the garden bed where you will grow your plants, it's time to test the soil. Testing at this point gives you a more accurate picture of the conditions the plants will have to deal with while they're growing and any additional adjustments you need to make.

The best time to take a soil sample is in early spring. That way you can get results back in time to add nutrients before you plant. Always ask for recommendations on how to treat the soil. Local garden centers might offer this service or seek out the local Cooperative Extension office.

The lab will analyze the soil sample for texture, pH, salinity, major and minor nutrients. Supporting information will clearly define the nutrients, how they affect plant growth and production, specific crop requirements, and other crop information. Recommendations address the amount of salts present and how to treat high salt levels. PH adjustments are rarely recommended unless levels are unusually high or low. Plant nutrient deficiencies are noted, along with recommendations of what fertilizer to use and how much to use.

If the recommendations are vague or need clarification, then by all means call the soil lab and ask to speak to the technician or agronomist who made the recommendations. They will do all they can to assist you in the process of correcting your soil and putting you on the path to growing bountiful vegetables and fruits.

Fertilizing Plants

Fertilizing is related to soil because you put the fertilizer in or on the soil, and the plants get the nutrients from fertilizers from the soil. Before fertilizing can be effective, the soil has to have the right properties to retain the nutrients from fertilizers and make them available to plants. If you've added compost, tested the pH, and adjusted it, and your plants still need more nutrients than those in the soil (and most edibles will), you can fertilize. More specifics on fertilizing materials, timing, and instructions are covered in Chapter 5.

CHAPTER 4

PLANNING & PLANTING YOUR GARDEN

Whether you have a plot of ground for a garden, are planning to retrofit your landscape to plant edibles, or you are growing some of your favorite veggies in containers on a patio, consider these points while you plan your garden. Be flexible. Gardens are ever changing, some areas will work out better than others and there are always new edibles to try.

Where to Put the Edible Garden

Draw the space to scale on paper, noting the overall dimensions and shape. This record will become invaluable over subsequent seasons to broaden or diminish the size of beds and pathways, design and install irrigation systems, add more containers, determine quantities of amendments and fertilizers needed and to order materials such as shade cloth, netting, fencing, hoops, and tunnels.

Provide sunlight and water. If you live in the colder climates with a short growing season, you want to situate your garden so the plants get maximum use of the sun. Visit the planned garden area at different times of the day to determine how the sun moves through the space. In the high desert regions, or in the case of container gardens, a bit of dappled shade can be home to many sun loving edibles and container gardens benefit from the cooling respite.

Planting edible trees or shrubs along a lot line is a good way to use this space and a friendlier way to mark the edge of your property than a fence.

With water shortages and short- and long-term droughts prevalent in the Rocky Mountain regions, having access to a hose bib is a must-have. You might be dragging a hose the first few seasons, but a hose bib can provide the source needed for a point of connection for an irrigation system later on.

Consider prevalent winds and micro-climates. Nearby fences and trees can block the wind and cool down soils with their shade and broad canopies, thus holding onto moisture a bit longer. Overhangs, walls, hardscape areas, and structures trap radiant heat, providing just a few degrees of added warmth during night freezes to the adjacent garden.

Plan for fencing, crop protection, and garden access. If you are in an urban area and do not have birds, rabbits, or deer to worry about, no fencing or netting may be needed. If you have any sort of pests, winged or hooved or pawed, then a fence is a necessity. Rabbits are in abundance in our rural area, so rabbit fencing surrounds our property. Deer munching in the garden can devastate in just one night of dining. An 8-foot or taller fence is required so that they can't leap over and browse. Plan for a fence first, then if you have to add electric systems later, the infrastructure is in place. If you have a fence, be sure to figure on at least one garden gate or entrance that is wide enough for a standard wheelbarrow.

Keep garden beds to a maximum of 4 feet wide and walkways narrow. Wider beds are difficult to harvest and to weed if you can't reach across without stepping in the bed. Narrow paths maximize the planting space. Twelve to eighteen inches for inner garden paths is substantial. A wider path (measure the widest implement you have to establish the main path width) along the outer edges or through the middle gives access. It is difficult to establish permanent pathways and beds until you have a chance to actually garden and harvest in the area. Likewise, wait a few seasons to install raised beds, just to be sure the layout is what you want.

Siting Fruit Trees, Vines, and Shrubs

Fruit trees, vines, and shrubs should be planned first. They are the largest at maturity and some will be in the garden for twenty to even eighty years. You can use the spaces under young tree canopies and intercrop between vines and shrubs so the space is shared. Plan for the mature size of the plants and allow for planting two if pollinators are needed. Pay attention to recommended spaces between trees to accommodate broad canopies and to harvest.

If you are retrofitting a landscape to edibles, plan for dwarf types as focal points, shrubs as green walls, and vines to cover a pergola or trellis. Once fruit trees start to bear, they can also be messy, so siting in open areas that can be mulched and cleaned up after harvest works best. If you have space for a small home orchard, keeping the trees in one concentrated area makes harvest and cleanup easier.

Plan to intercrop or companion plant among the fruits, in the veggie garden, and in containers. Native Americans intercropped rows of corn with beans climbing the thick stalks and squash trailing along the ground. "Three Sisters" companions shared resources. The beans, a legume, fixed nitrogen in the soil, the corn provided support for the beans to climb, and the squash cooled the soil and minimized erosion. Companion planting can be done in containers. A few shrubby basil plants make good companions with peppers and sweeten the fruit. Plant marigolds with tomatoes to ward off tomato worms and aphids. Carrots can be planted with tomatoes, cucumbers with nasturtium, lettuce can be interplanted with cilantro and radishes.

Plan for edibles in the landscape. Edible landscaping is the perfect canvas for interplanting edibles with ornamentals. Lawns can be replaced with dwarf fruit trees and herbs planted in the understories. Trellised tomato vines interplanted in the rose garden offer a deterrent to black spot on the roses. Pepper plants, closely spaced in drifts as midground plantings, provide a sea of deep green foliage and brightly colored fruit. Add shorter small-leaved varieties of basil to the front of the border. Creeping thyme and savory soften the edges of pavers. Various types and colors and textures of leaf lettuce make a great garden border, interplanted with nasturtium and pansies. The possibilities of combinations and companions are endless.

Once you've planned, it's time to plant! Here's what you need to know in order to select the right plants and plant them in the right places for edible garden success.

Growing Organic

The term *organic* means that the product has been produced or grown without man-made chemicals. Choosing to grow organic is a matter of preference. Plants grown organically usually have a lower impact on the environment because the growers focus more on building the soil, use biological controls as opposed to synthetic (manmade) chemical controls, and work within the natural ecosystem. If you buy organic, then try to garden organic as well.

Seed packets will indicate whether the plant is a hybrid or heirloom.

Heirlooms and Hybrids

Heirloom and *open-pollinated* are sometimes used interchangeably in gardening information. *Heirloom* refers to a variety that has been passed down through the years, having its beginnings before World War II. *Open-pollinated* refers to a plant that produces stable characteristics from generation to generation. Heirlooms are usually, but not always, open-pollinated but most always can be used to collect seed for use the next season.

Hybrids (F1 generation) are plants that grow from seeds produced by crossing two specific parent plants to blend favorable traits such as size, color, disease resistance, flavor, and more. Seeds from fruits of hybrid plants (F2 generation) can be saved and planted the next year, but they may not produce the same type of plants that they came from, so its best to buy seeds for hybrids each year.

Buying Local and Mail-Order or Online

Whenever possible, buy seed, plants, and bare root trees from your local nursery and garden center. They will stock and sell seeds from reliable sources, and smaller family run nurseries also try to buy from growers within the state. Local nurseries and garden centers know which plants do well in your area and that is what they will sell. Seek out your nursery professional for advice on types to plant, dealing with local soils, weather, and other cultivation challenges typical to your region.

Buying the Healthiest Plants

You want to choose healthy plants that will start growing as soon as you plant them (after hardening off) and that remain vigorous throughout their growth cycle. Some vegetables and fruits are prone to specific diseases, so look for plants with disease resistance. It is unlikely you will find diseased or infested plants in a licensed nursery since they are regularly inspected. If you do, point out the pest to the nursery professional so they can take care of the problem.

You can buy plants and seeds that have some level of resistance to common diseases affecting those types of plants. Look for these resistance abbreviations on the label:

BCMV: bean curly mosaic virus   **TMV:** tobacco mosaic virus
CMV: cucumber mosaic virus   **ToMV:** tomato mosaic virus
Foc, Foc 1: fusarium yellows   **TSWV:** tomato spotted wilt virus
PM: powdery mildew   **V:** verticillium wilt
PVY: potato virus Y

Look for these signs to determine that you are buying a healthy plant.

White, healthy roots growing to the bottom of the container. The roots determine the health and vigor of the plant. Pull the plant gently out of the pot to examine the roots. This is the equivalent (in shopper etiquette) to sniffing a cantaloupe or thumping a watermelon to test for ripeness. Check bare-root plants' roots as well. You do not want to see dark brown, black, brittle, shriveled, or mushy roots—all signs of possible root rots.

Green, new leaves or buds at the end of strong stems and branches. Look for a perky plant, standing tall with deep green leaves evenly spaced up and down strong stems and branches. You may see yellow leaves or yellowing between the veins of the plant, signs of nutrient deficiencies. If it is not widespread, the plant will immediately perk up when planted in the ground, but if you have a choice, choose the plant with the green healthy leaves. Discolored stems where they meet the soil, or branches that break easily may be warnings as well.

Select young healthy seedlings or plants that are in proportion to their roots and containers. When you are just beginning to garden, choose the healthiest plants for instant gratification. I admit that I am drawn to the price-reduced tables, swayed by the sad plants, long branches with yellowing leaves, pot-bound roots wrapping, and dusty dry soil. I adopt them and bring them home. Sometimes I succeed with the resurrection, sometimes not.

Planting the Vegetable Garden

Some plants are best grown from seed directly sown in the garden, while others are best planted as transplants. We have to start seeds early to plant as transplants for quite a few of the crops we grow in the Rocky Mountain regions, in order to fulfill growth requirements in a short growing season.

Directly sow these seeds in the garden. Some may be listed under transplants too. For specific sowing instructions, see individual plant profiles: Bean, carrot, chives, cucumber, dill, lettuce, onion, parsnip, pea, pumpkin, radish, spinach, Swiss chard, turnip, watermelon.

Plant these as transplants in the garden: Basil, broccoli, Brussels sprouts, cabbage, cauliflower, celery, chives, collards, eggplant, leek, onion, parsley, pepper, spinach, Swiss chard, tomato.

Starting Seeds Indoors

To get a jumpstart on the growing season or to grow some unusual varieties, you may want to start seeds indoors and grow them on as transplants. Look at the seed packets and in the individual plant profiles for information about when to start indoors.

You will need a few supplies to start: Seed-starting mix, seedling tray with cover or saran or bubble wrap to fit the tray, a soil thermometer, and a water source. Warm-season crops need heat. I have seen people use heating pads, but for prolonged use and regulated heat, select a growers heat mat with a thermostat. Provide bright natural light or grow lights to avoid stretching and to encourage good stem growth.

Fill the seedling tray with moist seed-starting mix. Place seed-starting mix in a bucket and moisten so that it forms a loose ball when squeezed but no water comes out.

Check the temperature of the soil with the thermometer. If it is too cold, set tray on the heat mat and warm the soil until it reaches the desired temperature.

Plant the seeds at the depth and spacing specified on the package. If you sow too deeply, they won't receive enough light to germinate.

Cover the seed with sand, vermiculite, or seed-starting mix. Do not bury too deeply, just enough to cover and to maintain moisture.

Label your seed tray/packs with the type, date sowed, and days to germinate.

Water the seed flat with a mist nozzle or spray water bottle. Cover with the plastic cover or with saran or bubble

Seedlings are fragile when they first sprout. Keep them moist but not soaking wet.

wrap placed loosely on the surface so there is allowance for air movement. Keep the seedbed moist and covered until seeds germinate.

Upon germination, move the flats to an area with bright natural light or hang the grow lights 2 inches above the seedling tray. As the plants grow, move the lights up so that they are no more than 2 inches above the plants. Keep the seedling mix moist but not soggy. Damping off (rotting or wilting of new seedlings) occurs when seeds stay too wet and cold while germinating. When plants have three sets of leaves, harden them off by moving them to a lower light level and off the heat mat but in a warm spot. After a few days, transplant to a pack or small pot in fresh soil.

Sowing Seeds Outdoors

Take the soil temperature before planting seeds outside to make sure it is warm enough. Sow fine seed as thinly as possible to minimize thinning. Sow larger manageable seed at the recommended finished spacing. Cover with seedling mix. Label each row or plot you have seeded with the type of seed, date sowed, and days to germinate. Keep them moist while germinating.

Hardening Off before Planting Out

Vegetable transplants grown inside a greenhouse or indoors need to be hardened off (acclimated to the change in temperature and light) before they're planted outside. Harden off purchased plants as well.

1. Place plants outdoors in a sheltered location and bring them in at night. Do this for a week. Water regularly and do not allow them to become water stressed.
2. Place plants in the open sunlight and bring them in at night. Do this for a week or until all danger of frost is passed. Water them regularly, checking for moisture in the morning and afternoon when small pots heat up fast.
3. After all danger of frost is passed, leave them outside all day and at night in a protected location. Do this for about a week. Water regularly.

Harden off plants by setting them on your porch or patio during the day and bringing them in at night until they are acclimated to outside conditions.

4. Move the plants from the sheltered location to a place where they will be planted for three or four days. Water daily.

5. Wait for a cloudy day (if possible) and plant in the early morning.

Planting Transplants Outdoors

Prepare the soil per soil test recommendations. Take the temperature of the soil to make sure it is warm enough. (The soil should be at least 60°F to 65°F for planting warm-weather vegetables such as tomatoes or peppers.) Plant transplants outside according to the spacing the fully grown plants will need. Plant so that the soil line of the hole and the soil line of the transplant are at the same level.

Some plants are best grown from transplants, including the broccoli being planted by this gardener.

Planting the Fruit Garden

Fruit and nut trees, shrubs, and vines are a more permanent, long living part of the garden. Because of their long tenure and their deep and far reaching mature root systems, it is also important to plant fruit trees and shrubs correctly to avoid long-term problems. Before digging any holes, have the soil tested so you know which organics and fertilizers to add. See individual plant profiles for specifics.

Fruit plants can be purchased as container-grown or bare-root stock. Plant container-grown fruit trees and shrubs the same way you'd plant a landscape tree or shrub, except you may be incorporating organics or other amendments.

GROWING TIP

Tomato plants and kale plants should be planted deep. Strip off all but the top two sets of leaves. Plant the entire rest of the plant below the soil line. Both of these plants will grow roots from the stem, making them stronger and healthier.

How to Plant a Container-Grown Fruit Tree or Shrub

1. Use a shovel or marking paint to mark the area for the hole. The planting hole should be two to three times as wide as the tree's rootball or container, but just as deep or even a bit shallower. Dig the planting hole.

2. If the soil test calls for amendments or pre-plant fertilizer, then thoroughly incorporate them into the native soil before backfilling.

3. Pull the tree out of the pot and run the blade of your clippers down through the roots at intervals around the entire circumference of the rootball. If there are wrapping roots at the bottom of the container, cut off the bottom 1 inch (1 gallon pot) to 2 inches (5 to 15 gallon pot) of root mass and then slice sides. If you eliminate this step, the tree roots will continue to wrap and won't grow out and down as they should.

4. Set the tree in the planting hole to check the depth. If the top of the rootball sits below ground level, add some soil, tamp the soil down, then reposition the plant. You never want the crown of the tree (the part where the tree trunk meets the tree roots) to be below the soil line. Backfill around the tree, tamping down the soil gently as you go to seal in soil around roots.

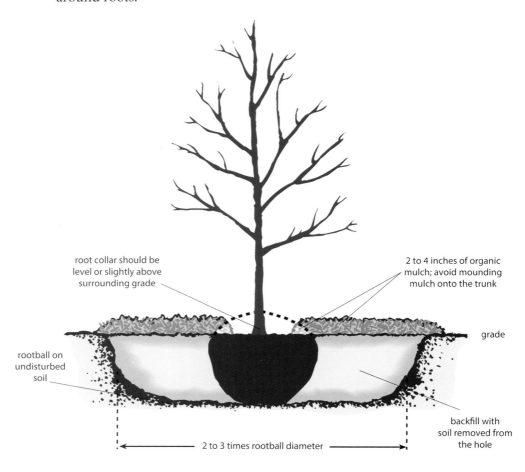

root collar should be level or slightly above surrounding grade

2 to 4 inches of organic mulch; avoid mounding mulch onto the trunk

grade

rootball on undisturbed soil

backfill with soil removed from the hole

2 to 3 times rootball diameter

How to Plant a Bare-Root Fruit Tree or Shrub
1. Soak the bare roots in water the night before you plan to plant.
2. Dig a hole twice as wide as the diameter of the root spread and just as deep as the length of the roots. Add and thoroughly incorporate recommended amendments.
3. Build a mound of soil in the center of the hole as high as the hole is deep.
4. Place the plant on top of the soil mound and spread the roots.
5. Fill in the soil around the plant, taking care that the point where the roots meet the trunk is above the soil line.

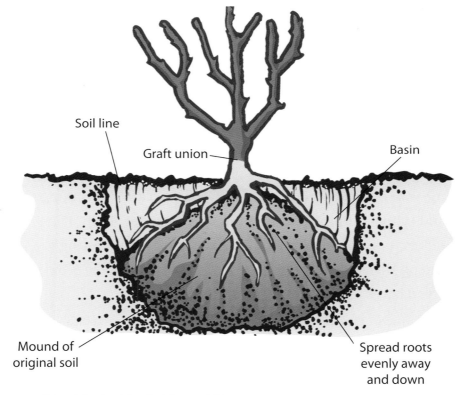

Water and Mulch the Newly Planted Tree
Build a watering basin to hold water then water the tree slowly and deeply. Fill up the tree basin with water. After it drains, check for settling and pockets that need more soil.

Plan to water newly planted trees every other day throughout the warm summer season. New trees don't need to be staked unless they're in areas prone to heavy rains and frequent winds. It can take a couple of years for newly planted trees to root all the way into the surrounding soil, so continue to monitor your tree for signs that it needs water.

Mulch around the tree, taking care to pull the mulch away from the tree trunk. Do not pile the mulch up around the trunk.

CHAPTER 5

GROWING YOUR GARDEN

Once the soil is prepped, the plants are purchased, and the garden is planted, your garden will do most of its growing on its own but will still need daily monitoring for water, weekly eradicating of weeds, occasional staking and tying, a thinning of certain crops, regular monitoring of pest populations, and hopefully, frequent harvesting to cap off the gardening season. A lot of worrying can be avoided if you have:

- Incorporated compost and rototilled or hand worked the soil before planting.
- Followed the recommendations of the Cooperative Extension agent or soil testing lab for pre-plant addition of nutrients.
- Planned and planted the "right plants in the right place", i.e. sun, partial shade, space to grow to mature size.
- Applied mulch.
- Provided access to watering or irrigation.

General principles of garden care apply to both fruits and vegetables, annual and long-lived types. Fruit trees and brambles have some unique issues and needs that are discussed further in Part II, preceding the individual plant profiles. If you furnish the plants with their most basic needs, then couple that with special care listed in the plant profiles, your garden will thrive.

This garden was thinned when plants were smaller to allow for adequate space for the vegetables to grow and spread out.

Watering wand

Garden Maintenance Activities

Watering

Water is our life's essence. We all need it to live. The edible garden cannot live by rainfall alone, especially in the Rocky Mountain regions that are in arid, low rainfall climates. Deciding when and how much water to apply depends upon the air temperature, amount of sun and wind, the maturity of the plant (and the root system), and the texture of the soil. If plants receive too much water, stand in water, don't get enough water, or receive inconsistent water, they become stressed, making them more vulnerable to pests, diseases, stunting, and decline.

Watering Seedlings

Seeds and seedlings need to stay continually moist while sprouting. They don't have very large root systems to absorb water. If you plant seeds in the garden, check them at least twice a day, morning and evening, to make sure they are staying moist. Water seedbeds with overhead water, using a hose with a mist nozzle that provides a very small droplet of water in an even pattern. This keeps the entire soil surface moist, while avoiding displacement of the seed.

Watering Trees, Shrubs, and Vines

Feel the soil with your finger to see if it is dry to about 1 inch deep. If it is dry, then use a hose with a water breaker and watering wand that regulates the flow and directs it evenly to the soil. Allow the basin to fill with water slowly, all the way to the top of the well. Newly planted, the plants will need deep watering whenever the soil dries out. In desert regions with hot summers, the first season's watering may entail deep soaking a couple of times a week to get it through the heat spells. You can also use a soaker hose with a hose end connector, wrapped around the entire tree just inside the tree well. You may need to run it for a couple of hours, once or twice a week, depending upon your soil type.

Watering Vegetable Gardens

After planting, new seedlings in the garden need a lot of water to get them through initial transplant stress and to encourage root formation and growth. They do not like their feet (roots) in a constant pool of water, but they do need the surrounding soil to be moist, or tiny root hairs will desiccate and die, slowing down establishment. We run the drip irrigation system for 10 minutes in the morning and 10 minutes in the evening on the newly planted garden. As the plants become acclimated, send out new leaf, stem, and root growth, and are well on their way to producing blooms, we cut back the watering to once a day, in the early morning hours for just 10 minutes.

Whether you water by hose, soaker hose, or with a drip irrigation system, monitor the plants daily, while maintaining a regular watering regime. Heat spells, high winds, and other weather episodes affect the schedule. Watch the plants for signs of wilting, changes in leaf color and luster. Always check the soil to see if it is dry before watering, then water the soil and roots, not the foliage. If soil is moist and plants are wilting, then they are most likely reacting to the heat (mulch to cool the soil or add a bit of shade cloth) or wind (provide supports if they can't stand on their own or cage them and wrap with crop protection cloth to buffet winds) and they will regain their stance in the cool of the evening.

Commit to Drip (Irrigation)

If you are making the investment in time, labor, and resources to grow your own edibles, then plan for a drip irrigation system, the best way to deliver water to the plants while conserving use. Sometimes trees appear to have "just fallen over" for no apparent reason. Upon investigation, the large mature tree has roots only in the upper soil level. This was caused by applying water to the soil surface when the tree was young. You can see how having a drip irrigation system for your long-lived fruit trees is so vital to building strong supporting root systems for a fruit-laden mature tree.

Lay a soaker hose or in-line tubing after you plant, while the plants are still small. Use sod staples to hold the hose in place.

There are many drip options available, and it is easy to switch to one or the other once you have the underground piping installed. To be sure, having a professional design and install the irrigation system infrastructure to bring you water where you want it is well worth the investment. Once the source is there, drip or micro irrigation systems are homeowner "user friendly."

Some of the basic types, terminology, and methods of delivery are:

Poly tubing: black flexible tubing that connects to the permanent underground pipe (PVC). It is used to move the water directly to the plant and is laid out on the soil surface, so you don't have to dig trenches everywhere. It comes on a spool or roll, and as it lays in the sun, it becomes quite flexible, allowing you to "snake" it in and out of trees and shrubs without kinking. Usually, mulch is applied over the tubing to protect it from degrading, from movement, and to disguise it.

Emitters: a term used to describe the method of delivery, like a sprinkler head, only the orifice is very small. Sprinkler heads deliver gallons of water per minute (gpm). Emitters deliver gallons of water per hour (gph). They are often plugged right into the poly tubing that is wrapped around a tree, shrub, or vine, evenly spaced so water is delivered to all areas of the root system. Emitters drip water slowly at a rate of 1 gallon of water dripping in one hour (1gph), 2gph, and up to 4gph. Spray emitters deliver the same small amounts of water but have the ability to send out a very fine spray, making them useful for seedbeds where you want the entire soil surface watered for germination.

In-line emitter tubing: This is poly tubing with the emitters spaced at 6-, 12-, 18-, or 24-inch intervals, but the emitters are inside the poly tubing and permanently fixed. Laser tubing is smaller and spacing between emitters is closer. We use 12-inch in-line emitter tubing in the vegetable

---

GROWING TIP

Before you head into the house after work, or before you get in the car to go to work, do a lap around your garden. Water any plants that need to be watered, and keep an eye out for pests or anything amiss. If you set a time to do this, you won't let garden maintenance get ahead of you, and you'll give your plants the best care. (Plus, it's fun!)

garden for tomatoes, peppers, squash, and cucumbers. We use laser tubing for closely spaced crops like lettuce, spinach, and carrots.

In the beginning of the gardening season, the tubing is easily pulled out of the way so we can get in the bed with the rototiller to prepare for the next crop. Then we just put it all back in place and plant. Tubing is made to resist breaking and cracking so it lasts for many years.

Mulching

Mulching all of your edibles cuts down on loss of water through evaporation, cools the soil and the roots, inhibits weed seed germination, minimizes mud splash onto the fruits, and protects the soil from wind. It is amazing the difference that a thick, 3-inch layer of mulch makes. Use it around the plants and in the paths too to keep the entire garden weed-free.

If you mow your own lawn and don't use chemicals on it, save the grass clippings—they make great mulch, and they add nutrients to the soil. Other good materials for vegetable garden mulch include: shredded newspaper,

Wood mulch in a vegetable garden

Mulching a vegetable garden with straw helps the soil retain moisture.

shredded bark mulch, compost, straw, and shredded leaves. Inorganic materials such as weed barrier cloth and burlap can also be used as long as water can penetrate the mulch.

When mulching around your plants, avoid mounding the mulch up around the stems of the plants, which can cause the plants to rot, but be sure to cover the entire soil surface between plants and to the edges of the beds. Mulch directly after planting transplants, trees, shrubs, and vines. For seedbeds, wait until seeds are germinated and plants are about 4 inches tall before you mulch.

Weeding

By definition, "A weed is any unwanted plant." Purely subjective on the part of the gardener. Granted, that opens the door to debate on native plants and self-sowing annuals that might take root in the garden and in other places where they weren't before. If I allowed Mother Nature to have her way in my garden design, there would not be room for anything else. Weeds are water hogs, space-stealing, pest attractants. Mulches do their job, and if you keep a watchful eye, you shouldn't have to spend hours upon end weeding.

Each spring, as the snow melts and the perennials start waking up, I look for the tufts of new green growth in the still barren vegetable garden, beneath the fruit trees, in the sprouting garlic bed, and at the base of trellised beds awaiting the beans or tomatoes. It's easy to spot the volunteer natives and perennial weeds at that time, as nothing else is growing.

Annual weeds start popping up at the same time as the garden seed. It makes sense, as they need the warm soil to germinate too. Annual weeds do not grow in a straight row, so as soon as the edibles send out leaves, errant annual weeds are easily spotted—and immediately removed. Check the garden every day and pull those unwanted plants, the weeds, when you see them.

I use herbicides in open areas, like gravel pathways out of the veggie garden area, driveways, sidewalks, and in landscaped areas where creeping perennial weeds Bermuda grass and field grasses are common. If your neighbor has these growing, chances are you will too. Use all your defenses to protect your crops, do it safely, and read all labels before applying anything, organic or synthetic.

Cultivate Your Edibles

Most of the plants in the garden are happy enough with good soil and regular watering. Seedlings need a little bit of attention at the start, then you can leave them alone until time to harvest. Some require more help as they put on growth, and once they are provided with support, they are happy to bloom and set fruit. Others grow and sprawl with exuberance but need a bit of protection as their large fruits serve as magnets for other critters wanting to nibble or chew.

Thinning

When you plant very small seeds, you usually plant more than you need, and they are sowed much closer together than they should be. Some crops, like leaf lettuce and spinach handle crowding, and you can thin them over time by snipping swaths of baby greens as they grow. Others, like carrots, have to be thinned by removing some of the plants in the row to open up

WHAT IS A WEED, AND WHAT IS A SEEDLING

Sometimes seedlings look like weeds. In this picture, you can see nasturtium seedlings (light green circular leaves) sprouting along the edges of the raised-bed box. In the center of the photo, next to the lettuce, are dollarweed plants (dark green circular leaves growing flat in the raised bed), which look like nasturtiums. Know what you're removing before you remove it!

Dollar weed masquerading as nasturtium seedlings.

These carrot seedlings will need to be thinned to leave at least 3 inches between plants in order to harvest larger carrots later.

space for the others. I tried to ignore this task the first year growing carrots, painstakingly sowing the tiny seeds as thinly as possible. The carrots never did well, not growing to their mature size, growing into each other and mutating. I have learned that you only need to thin once. Wait until the

seedlings are 4 inches tall before thinning. Be ruthless and thin to the final recommended spacing. With other crops that have larger, easy to manipulate seeds, save labor by sowing seeds thinly and to the recommended final spacing for the plants.

Staking

Some plants need direction to help them grow upright and reach the light. Others need support because their brittle stems can't support the weight of their fruits.

When tying a plant to a stake, line the stake up to the main stem of the plant. Then tie the plant to the stake, but never tie the string so tight that the plant is smashed against the stake.

And then there are some that want to sprawl and climb and crawl, but you lack the space to allow them the freedom. The best you can do, to avoid having to continually add stakes, tie limbs, and coax branches, is to install the stakes, trellises, or supports at the time of planting. Make sure they are strong enough to handle the load of mature plants and fruits. Check the plant's progress once a week to see what you can do to help. Staking and trellising is addressed in the individual plant profiles.

Fertilizing

Vegetables and fruits may need to be routinely fed (fertilized) in order to produce food for us to eat. Different plants have different requirements, which are listed in the individual plant profiles.

Balanced fertilizers have a combination of nutrients in them. Most of them have the "Big Three" macronutrients: nitrogen (N), phosphorus (P), and potassium (K). Some contain micronutrients such as calcium, magnesium, manganese, and iron. If the plant is showing deficiencies, and you have fulfilled any recommendations at planting time following the soil test results, then you may not need to fertilize again. The saying, "If it's not broken, don't fix it" applies.

TYPES OF FERTILIZER

There are many fertilizer choices available. Recommendations for additional fertilizers coming from soil test results should apply to synthetic and organic types.

Organic Liquid Fertilizer

Organic or natural liquid fertilizers are usually made from kelp, fish emulsion, or a combination of each. Mix these soluble fertilizers with water in watering cans to water into the soil. These fertilizers stay in the soil for a longer period and may build soil health over time.

Organic Granular Fertilizer

Blood meal and bone meal are organic fertilizers made from different mixtures of natural ingredients. Usually you will sidedress or incorporate them into the soil. They break down over time and feed the soil microorganisms and the plants.

Synthetic Liquid or Water-soluble Powder Fertilizer

Synthetic liquid fertilizers have macronutrients in them or are higher in single elements such as zinc and iron. Formulated for different types of plants, you can buy liquid fertilizers for houseplants, acid-loving plants, vegetables, and blooming plants.

If necessary, sidedress plants with organic fertilizers (sprinkle them on the soil alongside the plants) every few weeks to keep your vegetables healthy.

Synthetic Granular Fertilizer

Granular fertilizer is used for turf grass applications and for pre-planting. Only a small amount of granular fertilizer is needed. Granulars are usually applied with a spreader for even distribution and are followed with a deep watering to move the fertilizer to the roots to avoid foliar burn.

Slow-release fertilizers may be pelleted, coated, or encapsulated to allow for a gradual release of the nutrients over a period of months as the soil receives water. Slow-release fertilizers are often added to potting soil mixes, used as topdress for containers and garden plants, and also may be incorporated into soils at preparation time.

Nutrient Deficiencies

If your plant leaves are turning weird colors (purple, yellow), they might have nutrient deficiencies. Nutrient deficiencies cause highly predictable results, and it's usually possible to diagnose deficiencies by looking at the plant.

The diagram on page 51 shows the symptoms caused by the most common nutrient deficiencies.

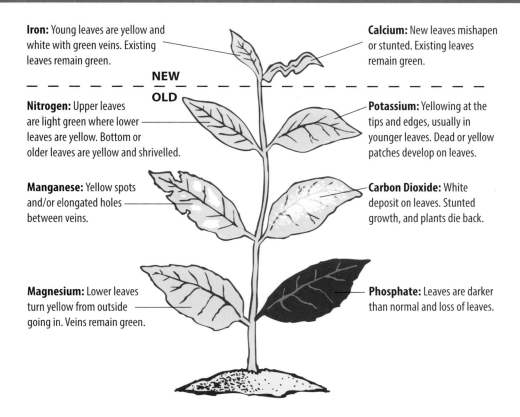

Iron: Young leaves are yellow and white with green veins. Existing leaves remain green.

Calcium: New leaves mishapen or stunted. Existing leaves remain green.

NEW

OLD

Nitrogen: Upper leaves are light green where lower leaves are yellow. Bottom or older leaves are yellow and shrivelled.

Potassium: Yellowing at the tips and edges, usually in younger leaves. Dead or yellow patches develop on leaves.

Manganese: Yellow spots and/or elongated holes between veins.

Carbon Dioxide: White deposit on leaves. Stunted growth, and plants die back.

Magnesium: Lower leaves turn yellow from outside going in. Veins remain green.

Phosphate: Leaves are darker than normal and loss of leaves.

Pests: A Fact of Life

If we start listing all the pests a garden can get, it would raise a panic that ends in gardeners running the other way. The gardeners' creed is, "Keep the plants healthy and the garden clean, and nature will take care of the rest." A few aphids, squash bugs, and munchers on the foliage of radishes or potatoes are not cause for concern. I often pick a tomato or a pepper where some worm has been there before me and just cut off the nibbled part, compost it, then eat what they left me. So prepare yourself to live with some pests. You'll still be eating the best tasting veggies and fruits you have ever had in your life.

Controlling Pests

Specific pest problems and controls are outlined in the individual plant profiles. For situations that you are not sure of, take infected or infested leaf samples to your local nursery professional or the nearest Cooperative Extension office for diagnosis and treatment options.

PART II

FRUIT & VEGETABLE PROFILES

Rocky Mountain Fruit & Vegetable Gardening is organized a bit differently than what you may be used to. To make the job of growing your own edibles easier, we organized this book beginning with the basics of gardening in our region, how to plan and design the garden, preparing the soil, and to finish off the process, planting and maintaining the garden.

Blueberries forming on three-year-old blueberry shrubs.

The plants are arranged by how you might incorporate them into the garden, beginning with the largest and longest living plants, which establish the foundation of the edible garden. The rest of the plant profiles are arranged by what season they prefer to grow in, so you know when to plant them and when they will be ready for harvest. The annual and perennial edibles will take up the remaining available garden spaces, whether they be in a space all their own or become part of the edible landscape. The perennials do not object to being moved but usually need a permanent spot to call home, while the annual types may be moved from season to season.

Botanical Names and Common Names

All plants (all living things) have a scientific name composed of a genus (first word) and species (second word). Those names are standard throughout the world, whereas the common names may differ from region to region, and from state to state. The scientific names of plants are also referred to as botanical names, and the language of them is known as botanical Latin.

Solanum lycopersicum is the botanical name for tomato. The botanical name is always italicized. Cultivars of tomato include 'Brandywine' and 'Cherokee Purple', among others. Cultivars are not in italics but are enclosed in single quotes.

Because different cultivars and varieties grow well under different circumstances, it's important to do your research before shopping. We've included recommended varieties or cultivars in the individual plant profiles.

In a few cases, mostly with fruit plants, there are several species of a fruit within one genus. Some species grow better in the Rocky Mountain regions than others. Blueberries are one example of this. That is also noted in individual plant descriptions.

Fruit & Nut Gardening, Chapter 6, leads off with a discussion of the fruits, organized by plant type: fruit and nut trees, shrubs and brambles, and vining and "garden" fruits. The size, type, and projected life-span of fruits and nuts determines where you plant them, when you harvest them, and which varieties will work best for your garden.

Vegetable & Herb Gardening, Chapter 7, is organized by cool and warm seasons. In the Rocky Mountain region, their season of preference has a direct relation to when we start the plant, when we plant, and when it matures and is ready for harvest. Certain plants will grow only during the cool season, making them perfect for cooler summers in high mountain regions. Warm-season crops may need to be started earlier indoors in those regions, but their growing schedule and love of summer heat makes them easy to grow in the warmer summer climates. Still others delight us by tolerating both seasons equally well.

Planting flowers around your vegetable garden will add color and attract pollinators.

At the beginning of each section, there's information pertinent to planting seasonal crops. Ideally, you can take the book to the garden center or home-improvement store, get what you need to grow a garden for the season at hand, go home, plant, and start growing.

Find Your Favorites

You can check the index at the back of the book, but you can also use the alphabetical list below to find your favorite edibles.

CHAPTER 6

FRUIT & NUT GARDENING

By definition, any edible that contains a seed is considered a fruit. A nut encapsulates a seed in its hull, so that would make it a fruit. Trees like peaches, plums, and apples all contain seeds, so that makes them, obviously, fruits. Zucchini, squash, and tomatoes all have seeds, hence they are called fruits. We chose to go with the official description, so in this book, the diagrams, care instructions, and other general information that refers to "fruit trees" is also applicable to nut trees, unless otherwise noted.

Peach trees laden with fruit

Choosing Fruits and Nuts

Fruit trees, shrubs, and vines take up a lot of sunny space in the garden in their mature state and are a permanent fixture in the design. Deciding what fruits to grow depends upon what your family likes to eat and how much they can eat. Some trees are self-fruitful, providing plenty of fruit for fresh eating. This eliminates the need to plant a pollinator, which takes up more space. If you plan to preserve the fruit, then having two trees of the same type is a reasonable use of space. Some trees need to have another to pollinate in order to produce any fruit at all, so you will need to account for their mature size and spacing between the trees in your garden planning.

There are many factors that influence the fruit plants you choose for your garden. When selecting fruits to grow at home, consider these points.

Source: Shop Local

Rely on your local nursery or garden center to select and sell those fruit varieties that do well in your area. They are the professionals and have the experience and the resources to offer selections that grow in our climate. The fruit varieties that they sell will fulfill chill hour requirements and have special characteristics such as dwarf sizes and pest and disease resistance. They will stock varieties that produce blooms later in the season to minimize late frost damage or fruit early in the season to allow you to harvest before first frosts. Once you have been successfully growing for a few years, you can branch out to other reliable resources to find some new and exciting fruits to try, but you'll have more long-term success if you buy locally when you are just starting out.

Consider Tree, Shrub, and Vine Size at Maturity and Their Longevity in the Garden

Planting a fruit tree or shrub is making a long-term investment in the garden. It can take as many as ten years to get a harvest from a nut tree that can grow to 50 feet tall and live eighty years. Most fruit trees bear (produce) fruit somewhere between two and six years after planting and grow from 8 feet (for dwarf types) to 15 feet tall. Some are short-lived to just ten years, and others can produce up to forty years and live much beyond that. When you buy fruits, the source (website, catalog, garden center) should be able to tell you when the tree will bear, how large it will grow, and how far apart to space plants.

You can purchase standard (or seedling) trees grown on their own rootstocks. These fruit trees can grow from 20 to 30 feet tall. Most home gardeners look for semidwarf and dwarf fruit trees. Semidwarf trees (10 to 20 feet at maturity) are best, if you have the space. They are usually

A fruit tree orchard shows trees in various stages of blooming.

longer lived, establish deeper roots, and have more disease resistance than dwarf trees (5 to 10 feet at maturity).

Vining and bramble fruits such as grapes and blackberries can be grown vertically but still need at least 6 feet between plants and require supports. Shrubs like blueberries need 6 to 8 feet between them. Before buying, decide whether you have the space for the mature size and can give it a permanent home for a long period of time.

Determine Time of Year for Bloom, Required Pollinators, Chilling Requirements, and Cold Hardiness

Fruit plants have to be able to flower in order to produce fruits. The time of year they flower is going to be affected by projected last frost dates in your area. For most of us gardening in Rocky Mountain regions, selecting types that flower later in spring makes the difference between allowing the trees to flower and set fruit naturally or having to provide frost protection for late frosts when the trees are laden with blooms.

Most fruit flowers need to be pollinated, and some need to be cross-pollinated with pollen from another tree. When selecting fruit trees and shrubs for your home orchard, pay attention to whether a plant is self-fertile or self-pollinating (in which case you can plant just one plant and still get fruit), or if the plant requires cross-pollination (in which case, you need at least two plants). If you have limited space, go for self-fertile plants.

For trees requiring cross-pollination, bloom time also matters. If one tree or shrub is finished blooming before the one you bought to cross-pollinate it, neither will bear fruit. Apples, peaches, pears, and other flowering fruits are categorized into groups based on blooming times. You need to plant at least two from each group in order to get good pollination and fruit set.

Chilling Hours Required

Fruit trees require a certain number of "chilling hours," or hours when the air temperature is below 45°F. Most fruit trees have chilling hour requirements that correspond to the length of time a plant will remain dormant before flowering. Chilling hours are required in many plants to trigger a break in dormancy, leading to blooming.

Temperatures above 60°F reverse chilling hours accumulated. If you plant a tree that requires 500 chilling hours in an area that receives only 300 hours, the plant will not flower and will not produce fruit. The following chart is an average for chill hours for fruits. Hours will vary with cultivar and variety.

In some of our colder climates, when cold hardiness of a plant is affected by single digit and below 0 temperatures, selecting plants that have been grafted and grown for their cold hardiness is important to their survival.

Chilling hours are discussed in more detail in individual plant profiles. Recommended plant varieties for each area of the Rocky Mountain regions have been selected, in part, with chilling hours and cold hardiness in mind. Your local nursery will also offer selections that fulfill chilling requirements and that can survive the coldest winter temps in your area.

Fruit	Chill Hours
Apple	400–1000
Apricot	500–600
Cherry	70–800
Pear	400–500
Peach	600–800
Plum	400
Blackberry	200–500
Blueberry	800
Grape	100
Raspberry	700–800
Hazelnuts	800
Pecan	300–500
Walnut	600–700

Determine If the Types You Choose Have Pest and Disease Resistance

Fruit trees and shrubs are susceptible to an alarming number of pest and disease problems. There are sprays and treatments that you can use to get rid of the problems, but you can give yourself a head start by choosing resistant plants. In grafted fruit plants, both the scion and the rootstock play a part in disease resistance. You will also want to know if there are warning signs you should be aware of, where you can go for help diagnosing problems and for recommendations of treatment.

GROWING TIP

The ultimate size of many fruit plants depends on the rootstock. Most fruit trees have two parts. The top of the plant, which produces the fruit that we eat, is called the scion. Rather than growing from seed, scions are cuttings from other plants of the same variety. The bottom of the plant is called the rootstock. Rootstocks can cause a scion to grow more slowly, increase cold hardiness, shorten the time between planting and fruit production, and add resistance to pests. The scion is grafted onto the rootstock, and the two pieces of plant grow together to form one plant.

The swelling on a tree trunk indicates the graft union where the rootstock (bottom) and scion (top) of a fruit plant grow together.

Consult Your Resources

The Cooperative Extension in your area will have lists of edibles, their individual growth characteristics, cultivation and soil needs, pruning and harvesting information. Talk to local farmers and other gardeners in your area to see what recommendations they may have.

GROWING TIP

If you have more fruit than you know what to do with, check with local food pantries, homeless shelters, and meal programs. Some cities have "gleaning" programs, where volunteers will come and pick your extra harvest and take it to a needy charity prepared to make use of it. Other food banks can accept and distribute your fresh produce. Don't let fresh food go to waste, if you can help it.

Apples ready for harvest

Planning a Fruit Garden

How many of each fruit do you plant? How much room do you need? The number of plants depends on the size of the plant, the yield you hope to harvest, and whether the plants require cross-pollination.

You can start small with two apple trees, four to six blackberry plants, four to six blueberry plants, and twelve strawberries.

Or you can tuck a few fruit trees along your lot line, add a row of blackberries near the vegetable garden, and devote a couple of rows or a raised bed from the vegetable garden to strawberries.

Caring for Fruits

Each type of fruit plant has its own specific schedule of care, but there are maintenance tasks that are important to all fruit plants. You will need to make time to take care of these tasks in your fruit garden.

Parts of a Fruit Tree

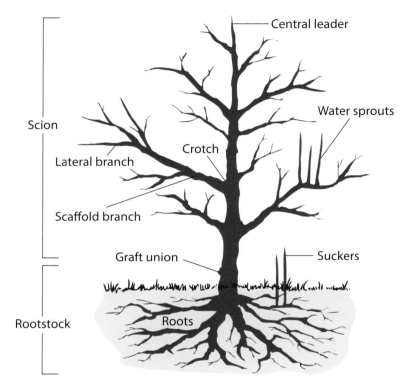

To understand the directions in the plant profiles, you need to be able to identify the parts of a fruit tree.

Rootstock: The bottom of the tree; the roots.

Scion: The top of the tree; the portion that produces fruit.

Graft union: The place on the tree where the rootstock meets the scion.

Central leader: The main trunk of the tree. (Apples and pears are pruned with a central leader. Peaches and plums are not.)

Water sprout: A branch that grows straight up from a scaffold branch on the fruit tree. Water sprouts do not produce fruit and should be removed.

Scaffold branch: A main horizontal branch from which fruiting spurs or branches grow.

Lateral branch: A smaller branch growing off of a scaffold branch. Lateral branches grow out, not up, and produce fruiting stems called spurs.

Crotch: The angle of a scaffold branch to the tree. Wider crotch angles are more stable and produce less breakage than narrow angles.

Suckers: Sprouts coming up from the rootstock. Sometimes suckers come from the stem below the graft union, and sometimes they appear to sprout right out of the soil. They should always be pruned off. Never put systemic weedkiller on a sucker. You can kill the whole tree.

Pruning

In addition to seasonal pruning of fruit and nut trees, grapes, blackberries, and blueberries also require pruning.

Most pruning is done in winter when plants are dormant. A few plants benefit from summer pruning. This is noted in the individual plant profiles.

PRUNING TOOLS

When you prune any branch, make sure you have the proper tool and that the blades are sharp. Small equipment maintenance shops can sharpen tools correctly. You want to make cuts cleanly, with no tearing or ripping of branches. Improper cutting can leave open wounds that the plant cannot compartmentalize (natural ability to heal), which in turn leaves entry points for pests and disease. Here are the tools that you need in order to prune.

A

B

C

D

Hand pruners

A Hand pruners have a cutting blade and an anchor blade. They're good for pruning small branches, under ½ inch in diameter, for deadheading, harvesting vining crops like cucumbers, peppers, and squash and for cutting small bamboo stakes.

Loppers

B Loppers are like big hand pruners. They have the same type of cutting blade but larger. Loppers also have longer handles. They're good for trimming shrubs and tree branches larger than ½ inch in diameter and for branches that are out of arm's reach.

Pruning saw

C Pruning saws fold up for easy toting in the garden basket. They are handy for cutting branches over 1½ inches in diameter or for any branches that cannot be safely and cleanly cut with the loppers.

Pole pruning saw

D A pole pruning saw has a pole pruner with both a lopper blade and a saw attachment. It is good for semidwarf or standard-sized fruit trees that have larger branches. The lopping attachment will have a string to pull to engage the cutting blade. With a pole pruner, you can reach higher up into the tree without having to climb a ladder.

PRUNING TECHNIQUES

Once the plants are in the ground, one of the most crucial seasonal tasks is pruning. Individual instructions for fruit tree pruning are listed in the plant profiles. Prune to control the size of the plants, to get rid of old growth and encourage new growth, and to increase sunlight and airflow. Pruning helps establish the structure of fruit trees and the renewal of vines.

Fruit trees are usually pruned into scaffolds (apples, pears) or in an open-vase shape (peaches, plums). The scaffold method establishes a central leader with branches that decrease in length as you move up the tree. The open-vase shape establishes several main lateral branches that bear fruit. You can use heading cuts, thinning cuts, and renewal pruning to establish these shapes.

Pruning stimulates fresh new growth that will produce fruit. Old orchards are brought back to life by careful pruning of the old trees. If you are in doubt of how to correctly prune, then hire a professional arborist. They will know how to properly prune for best health, structure, and harvest. Also check with the local Cooperative Extension for classes on home orchard pruning.

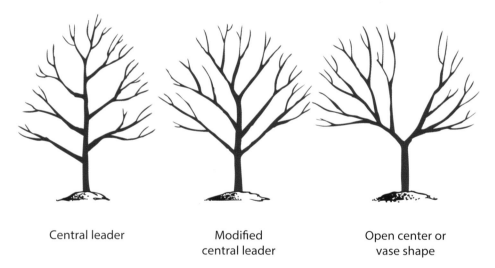

| Central leader | Modified central leader | Open center or vase shape |

Fruit trees are shaped by pruning. Apples should be pruned in a pyramid-like shape, while peaches and plums are pruned in an open, vase shape.

TYPES OF PRUNING

Heading cuts: When you cut off the end of a branch, that's called a heading cut. The response of the plant will be to produce more side-shoots below where you made the heading cut.

Thinning cuts: When you remove some of the "bulk" or interior branches by cutting them all the way back to the main branch, you're making thinning cuts.

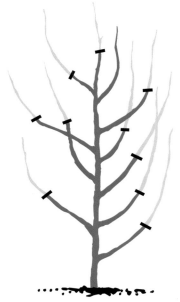  

Heading cuts involve cutting off the ends of plant branches.

Thinning cuts involve removing some of the interior growth of the plant.

Renewal pruning: This is a process most often used with shrubs, but which can also be applied to fruit trees, whereby you remove at least one-third of the old growth on the plant each year, stimulating new growth.

Renewal pruning is the process of removing one-third of the plant's growth each year.

Thinning: Fruit trees require thinning in order to produce larger fruits. The trees will self-thin about halfway through summer. You'll know this has happened, because suddenly a bunch of little fruits will be lying all over the ground. You can go through after this and continue to selectively thin. Pick fruits so that there is only one fruit every 4 to 6 inches along a branch.

How to Remove Large Branches

When you need to remove a large branch (anything that requires a pruning saw), use the following three-cut pruning technique.

1 Make the first cut on the underside of the branch, about 6 inches from the tree trunk. You'll only cut one-fourth to one-third of the way through the branch.

2 Make the second cut farther out on the branch from the first cut. Cut the branch all the way off. The branch will probably break off while you're cutting it. That is why you made the first cut on the underside of the tree—to help the branch break in the direction you want without stripping the bark off the branch.

3 You can see the finished second cut here. At the very bottom of the cut edge, you can see where part of the branch ripped. Do not make a cut that strips the bark off of a tree branch.

4 Cut off the branch stub remaining on the tree. Place the pruning saw just outside of the branch collar, which is the bark swelling between the branch and the main trunk. Saw through to remove the stub. Do not cut the branch flush with the tree trunk or you'll deter the tree's chances of healing itself.

5 In this picture, you can see that there's still about ¼ to ½ inch of branch left to allow the branch collar to heal. Never cover pruning cuts with tar, concrete, or sealant. The tree will heal itself if left alone. Sealant or tar creates a dark, moist environment that is perfect for bacteria to grow in. Sealing a cut can actually hurt the tree. If you follow this pruning technique, it will heal itself.

Staking and Support

Most landscape trees do not need to be staked when first planted, but many fruit trees do. Blackberries and raspberries require some sort of trellis to climb up for support. Fruits can be shallow rooted, which makes them easily dislodged by wind. Plan to stake newly planted trees and to construct sturdy trellising systems for newly planted vining fruits.

Other care considerations unique to different types of fruit plants are discussed in more detail in the individual plant profiles.

Pest Control and Harvest Protection

Fruit pest control depends upon the pest and the host plant. Some pests are controlled with a spray of horticultural oil when the plants are not leafed out. Other pests have to be controlled while fruit is developing on the trees.

Pest control on fruits never stops, because observation of the trees and plants never stops. Different pests are active at different times of the year. Make it a habit to cruise your fruit tree orchard and look at the plants. If something seems amiss, take a cutting or take some pictures and identify the problem. If you're having trouble, consult your county extension service.

GROWING TIP

Extremely cold temperatures can freeze flower buds. Some plants can tolerate more cold than their flower buds can, which means the trees might live through a cold snap, but the flowers won't. No flowers equals no fruit.

Temperature fluctuations also cause problems—mostly for plants that need to be cross-pollinated with pollen from another plant. These temperature fluctuations can cause plants to break dormancy and flower early. If you have three apple trees and one tree flowers early while the other two trees flower normally, the early-flowering plant can miss being pollinated. Don't be lulled into spring fever with warm spring like days. Do not resume watering or fertilize the orchard to encourage early budding.

Dwarf pear trees are easily managed from ground-level, as they grow no taller than 10 feet or so.

Growing Tree Fruits and Nuts in the Rocky Mountains

Growing fruit trees is rewarding, but it requires a long-term commitment, patience (it takes years for plants to bear fruit), prolonged good-health arboriculture practices, and vigilance in monitoring and treatment of pests and diseases.

PLANTING NEW FRUIT TREES

When planting new dwarf or semidwarf fruit trees, it helps if you can stake the trees. These trees are grafted onto rootstocks that can be more fragile than non-grafted "seedling" standard-sized trees. Staking the trees will keep them from blowing over in the wind as they're establishing their root systems. It helps to stake these trees for up to two or three years (re-setting the wires yearly to allow the tree to grow without wires cutting into the bark). Directing slow, deep irrigation to the root zone of the plant helps establish deep and wide root systems that will support the trees after establishment.

Standard pear trees grow much taller.

Find Your Favorite Fruits and Nuts

You can check the index at the back of the book, but you can also use the alphabetical list below to find your favorite edibles.

APPLE *(Malus domestica)*

With the right selection of variety, apples can be grown in the Rocky Mountain states.

I love our homegrown apples almost as much as the peaches, and the apples are much more reliable. I am selfish with my Jonagolds, barely thinning them as you should and not caring that my gluttony might give me lots of apples one year and few the next. They store, freeze, can, and dry well and no matter how many pounds we harvest, I never have enough of the crisp, juicy, little bit 'o sweet and little bit 'o tart beauties. There is an apple type for every gardener in the Rocky Mountain region to grow.

All apples that we grow today are actually two-part plants. The scion, a cutting that is grafted to the rootstock, is the top of the plant that produces the fruit. Rootstocks are selected to increase cold hardiness, shorten the time between planting and fruit production, and add pest resistance.

When you purchase an apple tree, you select not only the scion (or top), but often a particular rootstock as well. Nursery catalogs sometimes offer different choices—allowing you to purchase, say, a Gala apple with a dwarfing or semidwarfing rootstock. A "standard" tree is one that grows to full size without the benefit of a dwarfing rootstock.

The size that you select depends on how much space you have to grow the tree, the type of soil in which you will be planting it, and the average low temperature for your area.

Semidwarf rootstocks will produce trees that are about two-thirds the size of a standard tree and cut the time from planting to fruit production from ten years down to four to six years. Dwarf rootstocks produce trees that are half to one-third the size of a standard tree and reduce time from planting to fruiting from ten years to two to four years.

In order to get apples, you need to plant at least two trees that bloom at the same time so that they can cross-pollinate each other. Some trees are sterile and do not produce fertile pollen. If you plant one of those trees, you need to plant at least two others in order to get apples on all of the trees.

It is best to pick two trees that bloom at the same time to plant in your home "orchard" in order to ensure good cross-pollination. When selecting apple trees, you need to think about a few things:

- The size at maturity, how many apple trees you will need, and the space available
- Bloom time for pollination and the last frost date for your area
- Rootstocks and varieties suitable for your area
- Cold hardiness and disease resistance

Your choices will be easier if you consult the local Cooperative Extension and nursery experts for recommendations, purchase apple trees that are available at your local garden center and by carefully reading the cultivation information on the tag for what trees you need for pollinators. The garden center should offer those trees for sale as well.

Some Recommended Varieties for the Rocky Mountain Region
Colorado: 'Red Delicious', 'McIntosh', 'Jonathon', 'Fameuse', 'Golden Delicious'
Idaho: 'Earligold', 'Honeycrisp', 'McIntosh', 'Yellow Transparent', 'Spartan', 'Haralred'
Montana: 'McIntosh', 'Lodi', 'Goodland', 'Carroll', 'Empire', 'Haralson'
Utah: 'Earligold', 'Gala', 'Sweet Sixteen', 'Jonagold', 'Gold Rush', 'Yellow Transparent'
Wyoming: 'Bramley's Seedling', 'Elstar', 'Haralred', ''Jonagold', 'Erwin Baur'

Check with the nursery where you purchase the trees on what types you need for pollinators. You will need to plant at least two apples in order to get good pollination. Some varieties are sterile and cannot cross-pollinate another apple tree. If you plant one of those, you need at least two others that bloom at the same time for fruit set.

▨ Planting

Apples are tree fruits and are planted the same way you would plant any tree. Refer to the instructions on pages 38–39. You should plant apple trees, purchased bare root or in containers, in early spring when they are offered and as soon as the ground is thawed enough so you can dig. It is best to avoid planting them during the worst heat of summer (mid-July through August).

Also important in terms of planting is spacing. Apples need to be planted close enough to each other for pollination. Plant standard trees no more than 75 feet apart, semidwarf trees no more than 45 feet apart, and dwarf trees no more than 25 feet apart. Plant trees so that they have room to grow without touching at their mature spread. (That varies from tree to tree. Read the label for expected dimensions.)

When planting apple trees, make sure that the graft union (where the scion meets the rootstock) is at least 5 inches above the soil. Stake grafted trees for the first two to three years to ensure that they take root and, literally, stay together while getting established in the garden.

Columnar apple trees are a great choice for small yards.

■ *Maintenance*

Once planted and staked, the primary maintenance concern is pruning. You need to water the trees as they are becoming established and fertilize yearly in spring by spreading a balanced slow-release fertilizer according to package instructions around the root zone of the tree.

To allow trees to establish themselves well, remove all fruit that forms during the first three years. (Difficult, I know, but your trees will be healthier in the long run.) Most trees will not fruit enough for harvest until the fourth season after planting.

Pruning is the critical type of maintenance for apple trees, though. From the moment you plant a tree, the way you prune it and train it will determine whether it is healthy and has good structure for bearing fruits or whether it is susceptible to breakage in high winds, breakage from heavy fruit loads, or low fruit production from lack of light.

Pruning to Establish New Trees

The diagram on page 73 shows how to prune a tree purchased from a nursery.

When pruning fruit trees, the goal is to establish good architecture. This allows air circulation in the canopy (top of the tree), permits light penetration (sunlight must reach the inner branches for fruit production), and creates a branch structure that can withstand wind and the weight of fruit on a branch.

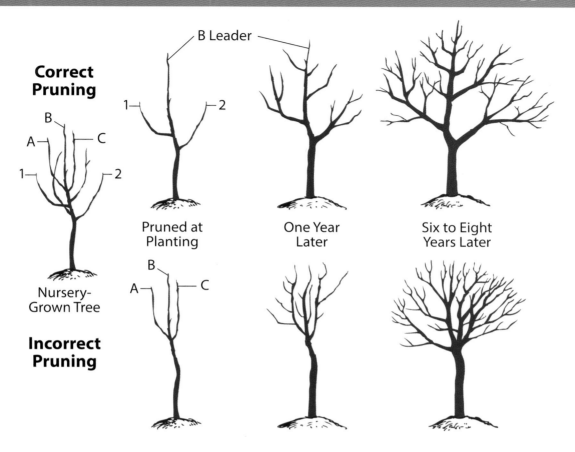

Correct Pruning

B
A — — C
1 — — 2

Nursery-Grown Tree

Incorrect Pruning

B Leader

1 — — 2

Pruned at Planting

One Year Later

Six to Eight Years Later

B
A — — C

Pruning to Maintain Established Trees

Once the tree has become established (four or more years), you'll need to prune to maintain good architecture and encourage fruiting. Always remove water sprouts, which are branches that grow straight up from side branches. These aren't growing in the right direction to produce good long-term shape.

In addition to structural maintenance, you'll prune to encourage fruiting. Some apple trees produce fruits from spurs, which are small, compressed,

Apple tree spur

nubby stems along the branches. It's a rule of thumb that the fewer fruits there are on the tree, the bigger the fruits will be. If there are too many spurs on the tree, you can use hand pruners to simply snip off the spurs at even intervals. If the tree doesn't have enough spurs, you can cut off the end of the branch, which will cause the plants to sprout more spurs along the branches. Some apples bear fruit from the tips of branches. Prune these trees by cutting back the ends of branches by 8 to 10 inches, leaving five or six buds on the branches.

The overall guiding principle of pruning all fruit trees is to maintain a somewhat triangular shape. This allows light to reach every part of the tree. (Remember that no light equals no fruit.)

■ *Pest Problems*

Apples are members of the rose family (along with many other edible fruit plants), and are susceptible to a wide variety of pests and diseases. Anthracnose, apple scab, powdery mildew, and fire blight are some of the worst diseases of apples. Try to plant cultivars that are resistant to these diseases. Spraying dormant oil during winter can control many diseases. Apple maggots are the worst insect pests. To control apple maggots, hang traps in the trees—these are available in garden centers and home-improvement stores. You can also protect individual fruits by placing a plastic bag around each fruit and attaching it with a clothespin.

If you have trouble identifying what pest, disease, or cultural problem (caused by maintenance or lack thereof rather than an insect or disease) is plaguing your apple tree, take pictures, including close-ups, and cut a branch and take it to your County Extension Service.

Apple scab

Cedar apple rust

■ *Harvesting*

Apples are ready for harvest when they easily come off the tree in your hand. Twist the apple until it breaks away from the stem. Avoid ripping, as you can damage the spurs or buds that will produce fruit next year.

Days from Bloom to Harvest for Commonly Grown Apples

Variety	Days from bloom to harvest
Earligold	105
Gala	105
Golden Delicious	155
Haralred	135
Honeycrisp	135
Lodi	65
McIntosh	130
Yellow Transparent	100

GROWING TIP

Apple trees will self-thin in early summer. Do not be alarmed when you see some of the fruits drop off the tree. It's a natural process that will result in larger fruits ripening in fall.

Pick up dropped fruits, and rake and remove leaves each year.

Certain apple diseases will overwinter in dead leaves and fruits.

Control pests by practicing good garden hygiene.

APRICOT *(Prunus armeniaca)*

We had the first harvest of 'Tilton' apricots four years after planting the bare-root tree. They all came ripe at once, seemingly overnight, turning a golden peachy hue, and when we gave them a little squeeze, there was just the slightest give to the fruit. We filled buckets with 23 pounds of delicious juicy fruits, while the bees buzzed in anger at us taking the sugar-filled apricots away from them so quickly. They keep well refrigerated, but with so many, we cut them in half, pulled out the seed, and put them cut side down on racks in the food dehydrator for about 72 hours. Dried this way, they store for up to a year, but they never made it that long, as I love the dried fruit more than freshly picked right off the tree.

■ *Recommended Varieties*

Apricots are more cold-hardy than peaches, but bloom early, subjecting them to late frosts causing the flowers to abort. Choose late season bloomers, situate the trees on slopes away from down pockets or alongside buildings for warmth and protection. Buy from your local nursery and consult the Cooperative Extension for variety and cultivation recommendations.

'Mormon' is self fertile, hardy to Zone 4, blooms late, early bearing. 'Tilton' is hardy, resistant to light frost, self fertile. 'Sungold' is smaller to 15 feet, hardy, developed in Minnesota and high in sugar. *P. a. mandshuri*ca, Manchurian apricot, is claimed to be the hardiest apricot with small size good for containers. 'Goldcot' is bred for colder climates. 'Floragold' is dwarf to 8 to 10 feet.

■ *Planting*

Apricots grow to 15 to 20 feet tall, dwarf varieties to 8 to 10 feet. Space 15 feet apart in a full sun location where they can live for 20 to 30 years. Plant as bare roots in early spring in a well-draining soil amended with compost. For bare root planting information, see page 39.

■ *Maintenance*

Apply complete fertilizer in spring, but use one low in nitrogen to encourage flower and fruit. Fertilize containerized trees again a couple of months later. Apply water slowly and deeply, keeping soil moist through harvest, then cut back on water to deep but infrequent watering, allowing the soil to dry between waterings.

Thin fruit in mid-spring so that they are 2 to 3 inches apart on the branch. Prune apricots after harvest to avoid wound-spreading diseases. Prune for an open center.

Pest Problems

Apricots are subject to verticillium. Plant in areas that have not recently had tomatoes, peppers, eggplant, berries, or potatoes. For other problems, contact the Cooperative Extension for diseases to watch for and preventative measures. The birds will peck at the fruits. Use netting when you start to see blush of color. Harvest as soon as they are ripe.

Harvesting

When fully mature, one tree can give over 100 pounds of fruit. Harvest when fruit is colored and just a bit soft when squeezed. Apricots dry well.

An apricot tree in full bloom.

CHERRY *(Prunus avium, Prunus cerasus)*

Apparently, the squirrel and chipmunks love our cherries as much as we do. However, they do not wait until the jewels ripen, stealing and carrying them off even before the birds are interested. We use orchard netting, encapsulating the entire tree and pinning the webbing down to the ground as soon as we see the clusters of hard, green juvenile fruits hanging from the trees. We will go to any lengths to save our cherries and they are well worth the extra trouble. Cherries that make it to the kitchen—as we eat them while we pick—can, freeze, and dry well.

■ *Recommended Varieties*

There are tart cherries and sweet cherries. Some sweet cherries are self-fertile and do not require a pollinator tree. Others do require cross-pollination, so make sure to pick out compatible varieties (bloom at the same time) when shopping. Sweet cherries are hardy in warmer areas, tolerant to USDA Zones 5 and above. Most tart cherries are self-pollinating and are very cold hardy, so they are good for our colder Rocky Mountain regions.

All regions can grow tart cherries, 'Montmorency', 'Meteor', and 'Northstar'.

Recommended sweet cherries are as follows. Check with your local Cooperative Extension and garden centers for availability of varieties and pollinators.

Tart cherries grow well in many parts of the Rocky Mountain states.

GROWING TIP

Cherry trees don't need a lot of fertilizer. However, if trees are growing less than 10 inches a year, they'll benefit from an application of a balanced orchard fertilizer.

Colorado: 'Sweetheart', 'Lapins', 'Stella', 'Columbia', 'Benton'
Idaho: 'Bing', 'Chelan', 'Hartland', 'Stark Gold', 'Hedelfinger', 'Royal Ann'
Montana and Wyoming: 'Bing', 'Early Burlat', 'Black Tartarian'
Utah: 'Bing', 'Black Tartarian', 'Stella', 'Royal Ann', 'Utah Giant'

Planting

Cherries grow best in full sun and well-drained soil. Plant the trees, taking care to ensure that the graft union is at least 3 inches above the soil. Follow instructions for planting trees on pages 38–39. Stake the trees for the first two years after planting.

Maintenance

Cherry trees are highly susceptible to drought. Water the trees daily after planting and do not let them dry out. Mulch around newly planted trees to keep moisture in around the root zone.

Tart cherry pruning is similar to peach tree pruning, in terms of shape. You'll prune tart cherries to an open vase shape or semi-open vase shape. Prune sweet cherries as you'd prune an apple. Cherries fruit on spurs, like apples, so treat individual branches as you would apple trees, being careful not to knock off or break off the spurs.

Prune cherry trees in mid-summer.

Pest Problems

There are some diseases that affect cherry trees, but they usually do not cause problems for the home gardener. Just take care to rake away all leaf and fruit debris at the end of the season so that disease spores can't overwinter right under the tree.

Birds are one of the most annoying pests of cherry trees. You can cover smaller trees with bird netting, but if you have a larger tree, hang a "scary eye" balloon in the tree (a yellow beach ball with red circles with black centers) to scare the birds away.

Harvesting

Cherries are ready to harvest when they easily fall off the tree. Sweet cherries will be firm, while tart cherries will be starting to soften.

PEACH & NECTARINE *(Prunus persica)*

It is cause for celebration when the peach and nectarine trees have made it through their flowering cycle, past late frosts (and even snowfall!) and we find small green fruits hiding out under the dense foliage in mid-summer. A lot of gardeners grow peaches here, and we all go through the agony of Mother Nature's defeat with a set of the jaw and a claim that next season will be better. And when it is, we share our recipes and blue-ribbon cobblers, pies, jarred peaches and preserves at the local Peach Days Festival.

Peach

■ Recommended Varieties

For most regions in the Rocky Mountain states, cold hardiness and late last frost dates are critical for peach and nectarines. Hardy in warmer Zones 5 and above, yet having enough chill hours to perform are 'Elberta', 'Hale Haven', 'Belle of Georgia', 'May Gold', and 'Red Haven'. In colder climates try 'Contender', 'Canadian Harmony', 'Harbrite', 'Eden', 'Reliance', and 'Ranger'.

Nectarines, hardy to Zone 5, are 'Arctic Fantasy', 'Fantasia', 'Ruby Grand', and 'Sun Red'.

■ Planting

Plant peaches in early spring. Peaches and nectarines are self-fertile, so spacing is not as critical when planting these trees. Location is important. Peaches are susceptible to cold snaps. Plant these trees near the top of a hill or slope so that cold air can drain down and away from the trees.

Peaches and nectarines need well-drained soil to establish healthy root systems. They are not at all tolerant of heavy, poorly drained soils.

Follow instructions for planting trees on pages 38–39, and stake peaches and nectarines for the first two years after planting.

■ Maintenance

Peaches are fast growers that do not need extra fertilizer, except in sandy soils. The biggest aspects of peach maintenance are pruning, thinning, and pest control. Prune peach trees to maintain an upright vase shape. Peaches produce lots of side branches, about half of which need to be removed yearly in order to channel energy into production of fewer, larger fruits. Peaches will self-thin in summer, dropping as many as half of the fruits. You can further thin peaches, leaving one peach or nectarine to mature every 4 to 6 inches along the branch.

To keep peaches productive (they produce fruit on one-year-old branches), prune after the plants have finished fruiting and you have finished harvesting to remove any water sprouts.

Pest Problems

Nectarine

Give yourself a leg up on pest control by planting resistant varieties. Even this won't spare your plants from all pests. If you want to grow fresh peaches and nectarines, you will have to follow a pest-control program. Whether you use organic or synthetic pesticides is up to you, but you won't have peaches without being vigilant about pests.

Diseases are a bigger problem than insects with peaches and nectarines. Peach leaf curl, brown rot, peach scab, bacterial spot, and other diseases are problems with peaches. The main insect pest is plum curculio. Use fungicides and dormant oil in spring before the plants bloom in order to control diseases. Use a properly labeled insecticide to treat plum curculio right after blossom drop to treat this insect.

Harvesting

Peaches are ready for harvest starting in early summer and continuing through late summer, depending on the variety. The fruits should easily come off the tree without yanking, and they should be slightly soft to the touch.

GROWING TIPS

Be prepared to replace your peach and nectarine trees. They're both short-lived, and you'll be lucky to get at least seven productive years out of these fruit trees.

Remove fruits that form on the plant for the first three years. That will allow the plants to put all of their energy into growing and establishing healthy roots.

PEAR *(Pyrus* spp.*)*

We planted our Bartlett, Anjou, and Bosc Red pear trees in early spring 2010 from bare-root plants. We had our first few pears ripen for picking in summer of 2013. The dwarf types that are late season bloomers work best for us, as we most likely get hit with winter-like

Espaliered pear tree

freezes, storms, and even snowfall in mid-March to the end of April. The smaller trees make it possible for us to wrap the trees in crop protection cloth to keep the blooms from aborting. Orchard netting easily goes over the tops of the trees and down to the ground, keeping birds at bay. Pears can be space savers in the edible landscape in dwarf sizes and make great espaliers to line pathways.

■ *Recommended Varieties*

European types are the most cold hardy: 'Bartlett', 'Flemish Beauty', 'Luscious', 'Parker', 'Patten'

In warmer regions, Zone 5 and above, try 'Harrow Delight', 'Warren', 'Bosc', 'D'Anjou', 'Moonglow'

■ *Planting*

Plant pears in full sun in well-drained, nutrient-rich soil in early spring. Add compost to the planting hole and use compost as a mulch around the plants. Plant two or more trees, 10 to 15 feet apart, so that they can cross-pollinate each other. While most Asian pears are self-fertile, they'll produce a bigger harvest if they have a cross-pollinating tree nearby.

■ *Maintenance*

Pears need deep slow watering during the growing season. They rarely need extra fertilizer except in extremely poor sandy soil. As with other fruit trees, pruning is the most important aspect of maintenance (beyond pest control).

Prune pears in late winter in a similar manner to apple trees—to encourage airflow and light penetration. Maintain a triangular shape with a strong central leader (single central trunk) and scaffold (layers of branches that progressively get shorter toward the top of the tree).

Pears bear fruit on three- to ten-year-old spurs. Do not prune to remove spurs, as making more pruning cuts will open more areas for diseases to attack the plants. You will want to renewal prune by removing at least 10 percent of the canopy each year to promote new growth. Also be sure to remove water sprouts and root suckers.

Pears bear fruit in clusters. To encourage production of fewer, larger fruits, thin fruits when they're 1 inch in diameter, leaving one fruit per cluster with clusters spaced every 6 inches along each branch.

Pest Problems

Fire blight is the biggest problem in fire-blight-prone areas. You'll know that your tree has a fire blight problem if the leaves on specific branches turn brown and dry up, seemingly overnight. Do not overfertilize or overprune, plant resistant varieties, and practice good plant hygiene. You can control insect problems that affect pears, such as the aphid-like pear psylla, by spraying trees with dormant oil during winter.

Harvesting

Pears will be ready to harvest 100 to 140 days after flowering, depending on the variety. European pears will not ripen fully on the tree so need to be harvested when they are still firm to the touch. Then allow them to soften indoors.

It can take several years for a pear tree to bear fruit.

GROWING TIPS

Pear trees can have narrow branch angles that make the branches susceptible to breaking from high winds or heavy fruit loads. You can train the branches to have a wider angle by hanging weights on the individual branches when they are young and flexible. That sounds weird, but it works. If you have space along a wall, you can espalier a pear tree to grow flat against a trellis.

Keep in mind, some pears can take ten to twelve years to start bearing fruit, but they are long-lived trees. Be patient.

PECAN *(Carya illinoinensis)*

There are many pecan groves in our area, so while our pecan is just a small sapling and years away from producing, we have local farmers to turn to. Pecan trees grow large and have broad beautiful shade canopies, really the main reason we planted ours where summer shade is always welcomed. They will produce a light crop of nuts without another cross-pollinator and they take up a huge amount of space, so plan accordingly. When I drive by the grove of pecan trees in the summer, the temperature immediately drops by at least 10°F—a drop that feels instantly cool in our triple-digit summer heat. The nuts they produce and their shells that I find in local compost are bonuses!

■ *Recommended Varieties*

Pecans require cross-pollination from another variety of tree to produce substantial harvests. If you live in warm summer areas, Zones 4 and above, and have a large space that pecans would be allowed to grow, then it's worth reviewing pecan selection information with your Cooperative Extension before purchasing. Here are a few suggestions, though.

'Pawnee', a small pecan (30 feet × 30 feet) and 'Posey' are hardy and pollinate each other. They are hardy in Zones 6 to 9. 'Stark Surecrop' and 'Starkings Hardy Giant' pollinate 'Colby'. Northern Hardy Pecan is reported to tolerate temps to minus 30°F, growing in Zones 4–9, takes 120–140 days to mature.

Container-grown trees are faster to establish than bare-root trees and can be planted at any time but not in the heat of summer. Do not purchase a container-grown tree that is larger than 5 or 6 feet tall. Pecans establish taproots as they grow, which makes them hard to transplant. Bare-root trees should be planted outside in early spring.

Pecan trees are large, full-sized landscape trees.

Planting

Pecan trees are large, so plant them where they have room to grow to heights of 40 to 50 feet. Be careful to avoid planting under power lines. Plant pecan trees 60 to 80 feet apart.

Maintenance

Mulch trees with compost, and water frequently (at least 10 to 15 gallons per week) when trees are first establishing themselves. Test the soil where pecan trees are growing to ensure proper levels of zinc. Zinc deficiency can cause bronzing and mottling of leaves; early defoliation; dead twigs in tops of trees; abnormally small nuts; small yellowish, chlorotic leaves; and short, thin twigs growing on older scaffold branches, with rosettes of small, yellowish green leaves at the tips.

Pest Problems

Squirrels are one of the worst pests affecting pecan trees. This is primarily because they eat your harvest before you can. To protect trees from squirrels, wrap the trunk with a metal shield, 5 feet off the ground. You can attach the shield with spikes that you withdraw slightly each year as the tree grows.

Pecan scab is a major disease problem for pecans. You can mostly control the spread of this disease by cleaning up leaves, twigs, and nuts from the previous year and throwing them away (not composting).

Pecans can be eaten fresh or used in cooking and baking.

Harvesting

Start harvesting nuts when they start to fall. Lay a clean sheet under the trees and shake the branches to loosen the nuts. Once you harvest them from the tree, lay them in a single layer in a warm, dry place to dry out. You can freeze nuts in resealable plastic bags until you're ready to use them.

PLUM *(Prunus* spp.*)*

We planted our first 'Santa Rosa' plum in 2006, from a healthy bare root selected upon the advice of our local nursery expert, who had been running the family business for decades and growing fruit trees for even longer. 'Santa Rosa' are self-fruitful, so it was a good plum to start with for our small orchard. We have since added another, because the 'Santa Rosa', first harvested in 2010, fulfilled all our plum expectations. Delicious fresh and dried too. 'Santa Rosa' is a Japanese plum, commonly found in the markets.

■ *Recommended Varieties*

Plums require a cross-pollinator tree of the same type. Japanese plums cross-pollinate other Japanese plums, and European plums cross-pollinate European plums.

Japanese: The 'Santa Rosa' variety of Japanese plums is self-fruitful and doesn't require another variety for pollination, but you will get a heavier yield if you plant another. It is the most cold-hardly Japanese type to Zone 5. 'Late Santa Rosa' blooms a couple of weeks later, making it a bit more apt to hold onto blooms during a late season frost.

European types: Most hardy is 'Ember', and try 'Superior', 'Mt. Royal', 'Green Gage'

American types are worth a try in colder areas to Zone 4: 'Alderman', 'Superior', and 'Wanita'

■ *Planting*

Plant plums in full sun, 18 to 22 feet apart in well drained soils. Plums are tolerant of different soil types, growing equally well in heavier but well-drained clay soils and sandy soils.

■ *Maintenance*

Plums benefit from being fertilized once a year in spring right after they finish blooming. Because they're heavy fruiters, these trees benefit from regular water during summer while fruit are swelling.

Prune plums in much the same way that you'd prune pears—to let light into the trees, encourage air circulation, and create good branch scaffolding. Prune plums in late spring.

When fruits are ½ inch in diameter, thin fruits to one every 4 to 5 inches along the branch.

Fresh, home-grown plums make excellent eating.

■ *Pest Problems*

Plums are susceptible to a variety of diseases, including root rot, bacterial canker, brown rot, crown gall, plum pockets, russeting, and virus. Aphids, leafrollers, leafhoppers, borers, scale, and other insects can prey on plums. If your tree has a problem, the best way to get an accurate diagnosis and treatment is to take a sample to your Cooperative Extension office. They can give you tips about how to treat the problem.

■ *Harvesting*

Plums are ready to harvest when the fruits have a white, waxy coating. Allow European plums to ripen fully before harvesting. Asian plums can be picked when they are slightly underripe. Be careful not to yank the fruits off the trees, because you don't want to break the fruiting spurs, which will bear again the following year.

GROWING TIP

The biggest difference in growing plums from growing other fruit trees is that you need to prune them to favor longer, outward-growing branches as opposed to a strictly triangular shape. This results in an open center, allowing plenty of light penetration.

WALNUT *(Juglans regia)*

Walnut trees grow into large beautiful and stately shade trees that, in maturity, can produce between 50 and 80 pounds of nuts. If you are planting them for their ornamental and shade value, plant just one. Self-fruitful, you will still harvest some nuts in about seven years, but need not take the space to do it. They grow quickly to 40 feet tall and wide and are cold hardy to minus 25°F to minus 35°F. Two main types are grown in the U.S., English or Persian and Black walnuts. Black walnut is highly susceptible to thousand cankers disease, so are not planted as freely as they once were. English walnuts have not shown to be as susceptible. They are subject to late season frosts causing their blooms to abort, so select the most cold-hardy, late-blooming varieties and plant on a slope or area out of the way of cold air troughs. Walnut trees live to sixty years or more.

Walnut trees are self-pollinating, so you only need one of these large trees to harvest walnuts.

■ Recommended Varieties

Grow English/Persian types, most are Carpathian types and cold hardy. Look for 'Ambassador', 'Russian', 'Chopaka', 'Cascade', and 'Lake'.

■ Planting

Plant bare-root trees in spring in full sun. They are adaptable to all soil types, as long as it is well draining. Rototill in compost at time of planting. These are large trees that have huge shade canopies and drop their nuts when ripe, so plant in an open space where harvesting and keeping the trees clean will be easy.

■ Maintenance

Walnuts like deep, slow infrequent watering during their entire lives. For the first two years, apply water whenever the soil dries out, but do not overwater. They do not like to be continuously moist. After the establishment period, water twice a month during spring and summer, deeply and slowly to 2 feet deep, allowing the soil to dry very well between waterings. If there are spring or summer rains, then do not water until soil dries. Mulch helps cool the soil, minimizes moisture loss, and keeps the weeds down.

Prune when tree is dormant, but lightly to prune out crossing inner branches or to lift the crown to raise the shade canopy so you can walk under it. Do not top.

Walnuts do not need additional fertilizer after planting.

■ Pest Problems

The best defense against thousand cankers is to create healthy trees. Provide deep watering, keep the area free of weeds, clean up husks and nuts after each harvest to avoid canker.

■ Harvesting

The nuts and husks will fall from the tree in autumn. When the trees are small, you can shake them to release the nuts. If the husks do not fall off, rub them off with gloved hands or a wire brush. Lay them out to dry in the sun or in a dry sunny location for a few days, bag, and store.

Blackberries ripening for harvest

FRUIT SHRUBS & BRAMBLES

If you're just embarking on fruit growing, starting with shrubs is a good plan. Fruit shrubs are forgiving, easy to care for, and are prolific producers once established. Brambles (raspberries and blackberries) are the easiest to grow. Now there are even blueberries that are bred to tolerate less acidic soils and hotter summer temps. You might want to also experiment with growing less common fruits such as garden huckleberries.

■ *Landscaping with Fruit*

Edible landscaping is becoming the norm for those living in suburban homes with traditional landscapes who want to grow a little or a lot of their own fruits and vegetables. Even for those living within the confines of HOA's, the trend is catching on with those folks coming up with approved lists of edibles that can be substituted for front yard landscaping.

But even if you're on the fence about turning your fence into a tomato trellis, you can at least tuck some Swiss chard or herbs into the perennial border. The beauty about converting landscapes to edibles is that there is usually an irrigation system in place. That too, can be easily converted from high water using to water efficient drip and micro irrigation systems.

It's easy to work fruit shrubs into the landscape. Blueberries are quite ornamental. They have beautiful fall color—their leaves turn bright red—a plus for any garden. A fence of blackberries is somehow friendlier than an actual fence, and a melon vine trailing on a slope far surpasses a green expanse of ground cover.

■ Placing Fruit Shrubs in the Garden

Fruit shrubs can be planted throughout the landscape. Plant drifts of at least two or three near each other if they need to be cross-pollinated. Or plant a green wall along the edges of the property. Because fruit shrubs take up less space and throw less shade than fruit trees, you can also plant them in or around your vegetable garden. Plant taller varieties on the north side of the garden so that they don't shade other plants.

Get kids involved with gardening by letting them help harvest!

BLUEBERRY *(Vaccinium* spp.)

Blueberries are native to eastern regions of North America, where summers are cool, winters are cold, and the soils are acidic. Plant breeders have created more heat-tolerant blueberries that adapt to other soil conditions upon establishment. Getting blueberries through their formative years presents a challenge for Rocky Mountain gardeners, but with new hybrids available, substituting native backfill soil for acidic peat moss, adequate moisture, and acidic fertilizers, it's possible for all of us to enjoy plump, juicy blueberries loaded in fiber and vitamins.

■ *Recommended Varieties*

Northern Highbush blueberries are cold hardy to minus 35°F to as low as minus 45°F. and tend to be smaller bushes than southern types. Variations in bloom time affects the variety choice to ensure time for pollination and fruit production.

Try 'Friendship', 'Northcounty', 'Northblue', and 'Northsky' in areas with cold winters and heavy snowfall. The shorter bushes take snow load better.

Southern highbush blueberries are more suited to areas with less winter chill. Some blueberry varieties require a cross-pollinator. Check to see whether you need two different cultivars when purchasing. Select from each bloom time for continuous harvests.

Bloom Times
Early: 'Earliblue', 'Spartan', 'Patriot', 'Jubilee', 'Misty'
Mid: 'Bluejay', 'Bluecrop', 'Berkeley', 'Olympia'
Late: 'Legacy', 'Pink Lemonade', 'Darrow' (self-pollinating), 'Aurora' is very late

■ *Planting*

Plant blueberries in early spring in Rocky Mountain areas to get them established before winter.

Blueberries prefer a well-draining acidic soil. Our soil is

Blueberry plants provide fresh fruit in the summer and decorative foliage in cooler weather.

alkaline, so plant the berries in backfill soil made up of 75 percent peat moss. Dig a hole just as deep, but two to three times the size of the rootball and incorporate the peat thoroughly with the native soil before backfilling. Blueberries also need relatively high levels of organic matter in the soil. Add at least 4 inches of compost to the surface of the soil after planting and each spring thereafter, keeping it away from the main stem of the bush. Compost serves as a mulch, cools the soil, holds in moisture, and adds nutrients as it breaks down.

Maintenance

Water: Keep the soil moist but not soggy during the first growing season by applying water slowly and deeply. Drip irrigation fulfills both of these criteria. Blueberries are shallow rooted, do not like to dry out and cannot withstand drought. Use of mulches and good irrigation practices assures healthy plants.

Mulch: Help keep the soil around blueberries moist by mulching with pine needles, compost, or shredded hardwood mulch. Mulch to conserve moisture, control weeds, and to avoid cultivating around shallow roots.

Fertilizer: Do not fertilize during the first six months of growth. After the first season, feed with a balanced fertilizer before the plants bloom and after harvesting to encourage growth for next year. To maintain the acidity of the soil, use fertilizer formulated for acid-loving plants or ammonium sulfate (21-0-0) according to package directions and soil test recommendations.

Pruning: Prune blueberries in late winter or early spring. They produce fruits on one-year-old growth, so don't hack the plant to the ground as that would eliminate any berries. Prune a bit each year to keep the shrubs a manageable size. Renewal prune by selectively removing at least one-third of the branches each year (throughout the shrub) to encourage growth.

Pest Problems

Birds are the most annoying pest problem with blueberries. Throw nets over the shrubs once the fruits reach harvest size for protection. Deer love blueberries. Provide deer fencing at planting time. Consult your local Cooperative Extension for help controlling maggots and cranberry fruitworms.

Harvesting

Blueberry season runs from late spring to late summer in Rocky Mountain regions. Pick berries as you plan to eat them for the freshest fruits. (They can stay on the shrubs for a while, so no need to harvest all at once.) Taste a few to see if they are ready. Blueberries freeze well for long-term storage.

BLACKBERRY & RASPBERRY
(Rubus spp.)

Blackberries are easy to grow throughout the Rocky Mountain states.

It was a cold, cloudy February morning in 2006 when we planted the bare-root blackberry vines. As we planted 'Black Satin' and 'Thornless Boysenberry' blackberries, snow began softly falling on our heads. All we could do was chuckle at our situation—so absurd it seemed to us to be planting in the snow. We harvested our first berries, picking just under 20 pounds of the black jewels in 2008. In July 2012, we harvested over 70 pounds of berries from just six mature plants—mostly all 'Black Satin'. The 'Thornless' cultivar ended up not being thornless at all and kept reverting back to long arching stems covered in prickly nasty thorns. They have since been moved to obscure regions of the landscape, where hopefully the birds will enjoy them enough to leave our 'Black Satin' brambles alone!

■ *Recommended Varieties*

Blackberries
Trailing types are not as cold hardy as semierect and erect types. Trailing types are thorny; semierect are thornless; erect types are either thorny or thornless. Choose one that is suitable for your growing zone and the garden area. Know which type you have to determine plant care, staking, and training. Whether it bears fruit on first year or the second year affects when you prune the plant. Purchase bare-root plants from your local nursery. Blackberries live for twenty years.

Trailing: 'Boysen', 'Trailing Boysen' survive colder winters if overwintered under a layer of straw.

Erect or semierect: 'Chester', 'Black Satin' are disease resistant; 'Cherokee', 'Arapaho' can take the heat and cold.

Raspberries
Raspberries produce fruit in the fall on first year growth (primocanes) or in the summer on second-year growth. They grow well in elevations below 7,000 feet. There are some hardy to minus 20°F. Raspberries live for around fifteen years.

Trellising Systems for Trailing and Erect Blackberry Types

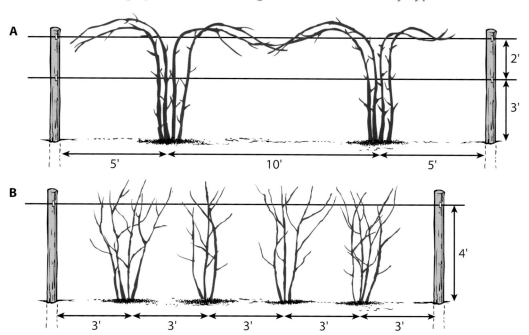

(A) Train trailing plants to a two-wire trellis. (B) Train erect blackberry plants to a one-wire trellis. Note that trailing blackberries need more space between plants than erect blackberries.

Train raspberries the way you'd train erect blackberries. For ease of maintenance grow the plants in a single line and train them to a two-wire trellis. That way you can easily cut back the older canes and allow new ones to grow.

Fall-bearing varieties: 'Bababerry' needs some winter chill but likes the heat, 'Autumn Bliss', 'Dinkum', 'Caroline', 'Summit'

Summer-bearing varieties are good for cooler summer regions: 'Boyne' is very hardy, 'Canby' is thornless, 'Chilcotin', 'Kilarney'

■ *Planting*

Plant blackberries and raspberries in full sun in well-draining soil. Blackberries are adaptable to most all soil conditions. Raspberries prefer a bit more acid soil, so amend the backfill with 50 percent peat moss before planting.

Plant bare-root plants as soon as the ground can be worked in spring. Soak the roots of bare-root plants for twenty-four hours before planting. Follow instructions on page 39 for planting bare root.

Erect or semierect brambles grow best with support. Stake individual plants or grow them against a fence. Set up a post and wire system with 2 inch × 4 foot posts and heavy-duty wire. Train the plants to grow along the wire. When they are bearing fruit, it is easy to pick up branches that are lying on the ground and flop them over the wires, their weight holding them in place without tying. If you need to tie the stems, use tree tie tape, jute, or twist ties.

■ *Maintenance*

Water: Frequent watering during the first year is the best way to make sure the plants get off to a good start. Run drip line or soaker hoses along the plants to direct the water to the roots. Water every two or three days during the first growing season. In subsequent years, water deeply at least once a week, giving the plants 1 inch of water per week during the flowering and fruiting cycle.

Fertilizer: Fertilize in spring when you start seeing new growth with a balanced fertilizer.

Pruning: Improper pruning of blackberries resulting in no fruit production has broken many a heart. Blackberry stems are called canes. A first-year cane is called a primocane. A second-year cane is called a floricane. Summer-bearing blackberries only bear fruit on second-year floricanes. Fall-bearing blackberries bear fruit on primocanes.

You won't hurt fruit production if you follow this rule: only prune blackberries all the way to the ground in fall, and only cut down canes that bore fruit during that year. The floricanes of summer-bearing blackberries

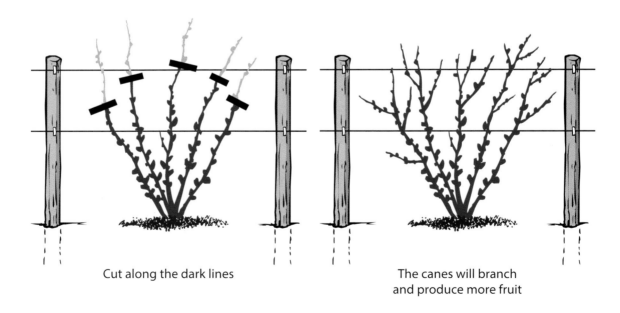

Cut along the dark lines

The canes will branch
and produce more fruit

If you cut off the top 6 to 12 inches of the canes during the first year, the plants will produce side branches that bear fruit during the second year.

usually start to die back after you pick the fruits, making it easy to see which ones to cut down.

Another type of pruning is to produce more productive side shoots. Prune blackberries back by 6 inches in the middle of summer after harvesting. This will encourage the plants to produce more side shoots off the main canes, which will result in a bigger fruit crop during the second year.

Prune raspberries by removing the fruiting branches in the summer after the second crop of fruit. You can also prune back the tips of second-year branches by 6 inches in the spring to encourage side shoots to grow.

■ Pest Problems

Blackberries and raspberries have few pests causing any major problems. Plant resistant varieties to avoid any diseases that may occur in your area.

Cane borers attack blackberries. You will be able to tell if you have these insects if the top of a first-year cane wilts and falls over suddenly. Cut below the wilted area and discard the branch with the borer. (Do not compost.)

Birds will eat your blackberries before you can. If they are a problem, throw bird netting over the plants.

■ Harvesting

Harvest blackberries when they easily come off the plants. The berries will lose their shiny sheen and become dull black when they are ready. Harvest fresh berries every other day for up to a month. If they are left on the vine too long, they dry up. Wash and dry the berries on paper towels. Lay them out in a single layer on a wax-paper-lined cookie sheet with sides. Put in the freezer overnight, then scoop into freezer bags to store frozen for one year. Berries also make outstanding jams and jellies.

Raspberries can be grown in the cooler areas of the Rocky Mountain states.

Grape vines need to have support in the garden, but they are well worth the extra effort.

VINING & GARDEN FRUITS

Vining fruits and garden fruits include some annuals—melon and huckleberry—and perennials—grape, rhubarb, and strawberry. The vining fruits, such as grapes, are sprawling with strong tendrils that allow them to attach to any support. Melons are similarly sprawling but are not as clingy in their habit and prefer to be left alone to ramble along the ground. Strawberries form a mass, spreading by runners that air-layer themselves when anchored to the ground, forming new plants.

This category of fruits includes plants that can be somewhat tricky to site in the garden. Some take up a fair amount of space over a long period of time, so need a permanent home, like rhubarb that lives and produces for over twenty years. Others, annuals like huckleberries and melons, are moved about the garden from year to year. The questions to ask yourself before deciding to grow any of these fruits are, "How much do you need to supply your family?" and "Do you have the space to grow them?"

If you are growing the edible landscape, grape vines trailing over an arbor form a shady respite, adding four seasons of interest. A strawberry pot or small bed of strawberries is perfect for condominium or apartment dwellers. Garden huckleberries don't get much bigger than a pepper plant, have much the same requirements, produce flowers and berries at the same time over a long season, and are perfect as a border plant or in a container.

Fresh strawberries have the best taste, but like to be moved every three years, so they do not have a long-term spacial commitment.

GRAPE *(Vitis vinifera)*

We grow 'Black Spanish' wine grapes and table grapes, red—'Ruby Red', white—'Niagara', and blue—'Black Monika' in our high desert, Zone 5 gardens. Grapes are an easy, forgiving crop. Select types rated to your zone, and they thrive in our lean alkaline soil, arid conditions, cold winters and, once established, can even take some drought. To add to it, they have very low fertility needs, actually balking at organic-rich soils. Grapes are an all-seasons interest plant in the landscape.

Grow grapes for both eating and juice or jelly.

■ Recommended Varieties

Buy grape vines recommended for your area from your local garden center. Also consult with the local Cooperative Extension for types, varieties, and cultivation needs. Here are some cold-hardy bunch grapes for Rocky Mountain gardeners.

Juice and jelly grapes: 'Concord', 'Catawba', 'Glenora'

Table grapes: 'Himrod', 'Lakemont', 'Canadice'

Red wine grapes: 'Black Spanish', 'Frontenac' is cold hardy to below 30°F and has late bud break.

White wine grapes: 'Frontenac Gris'

■ Planting

Buy bare-root and container-grown grapes. Plant bare-root grapes as soon as the soil can be dug in spring. Plant container-grown grapes in spring until summer heat sets in. Plant grapes in full sun in well-drained soil. Grapes do not grow well in heavy clay soils or soils with poor drainage.

Grapes require support. A post and wire system like you'd use for blackberries works well. Situate the wire at a height that's comfortable for you to reach—between waist and chest high. Plant grapes with 10 to 15 feet of space between each vine. Train grapes over an arbor, trellis, or fence for an edible green cover.

■ *Maintenance*

Water: Water grapes several times a week until established. Stop watering in the fall as soon as they start showing fall color or after harvesting. Discourage early season growth that might be damaged in a freeze, so even if you see buds swell, don't water yet. Resume deep regular watering in spring after the last frost. Give vines 1 inch of water per week as they leaf out and flower. When they start fruiting, cut back on the water, watering deeply and slowly (drip irrigation) once a week or if they show signs of wilt. Avoid getting foliage wet.

Fertilizer: Fertilize wine grapes according to soil test results and recommendations. For established table grapes, use a balanced fertilizer applied in spring as they are leafing out, after the last frost.

Pruning: The biggest mystery of grape production is pruning. Grape vines have a central stem, called the trunk, and two side shoots called cordons. The plants bear fruit from the cordons on compressed side shoots called spurs. Each cordon has many spurs. From the spurs grow shoots with buds that sprout and produce grapes.

Train new grape vines by allowing them to grow up toward the wire of the trellis. Cut off side shoots while the vine is growing up. Once the vine has reached the wire, cut off the growing tip to force side shoots to grow. Two of these will become the right and left arms of the cordon.

Prune grapes in late winter to early spring. At each spur, prune back all growths except for one piece of fruiting spur from the previous year's growth. Each fruiting spur should be about 4 inches long and have three to five buds on it.

To keep new fruiting spurs forming, each year remove every other spur down to the cordon. New spurs will sprout. Grapes bear fruit on one-year-old spur growth, so don't cut off that growth when pruning.

■ *Pest Problems*

The birds line the fence waiting for ripened grapes. Cover the vines with bird netting, your only tool for thwarting their efforts. There are some fungal diseases that affect grapes. Check with your cooperative extension if you suspect diseases.

■ *Harvesting*

Ripe grapes easily come off in your hand. Cut individual clusters as they ripen. Do a taste test to see if table grapes are ready to eat. There are other methods to check wine grapes for sugar content and ripeness. Consult wine making suppliers for equipment and resources on harvesting.

HUCKLEBERRY *(Solanum melanocerasum)*

We grow garden huckleberries, similar to the wild huckleberries in size and taste, but not related to them, actually being a member of the nightshade family. An annual shrub, reaching 2 feet tall and branching as wide, they can be grown throughout the Rocky Mountain regions, anywhere that peppers grow. Huckleberries cover themselves with deep green foliage, followed by bell shaped clusters of white flowers that set small green fruits ripening to black all season long. Fast and strong growers, fruit and flower are on the bush at the same time throughout the summer and into fall, making them a good choice for containers and for the edible landscape. A member of the nightshade family, all parts are poisonous. Don't eat the fruit until it is ripe and cooked.

■ Recommended Varieties

Look for garden huckleberry seeds, ready to harvest in 75 days. 'Chichiquelite', also called wonder berry, has a larger berry and heavier yield and can take some light frosts, even said to sweeten the fruit.

Huckleberries are easiest to pick when the entire cluster holds black ripened berries.

◼ *Planting*

Start seeds in the greenhouse or house, in January or February when you start the pepper seeds. Transplant to 4-inch pots, harden off before planting out in spring after the last frost. They are not as picky when it comes to soil temps, quickly leafing out in their native locale as soon as the ground thaws. Rototill in compost and site them in a full sun location, spacing the plants 18 inches apart.

◼ *Maintenance*

Water: Use drip irrigation or micro spray emitters aimed at the root zone to assure even moisture throughout the root system. They like a constantly moist well-draining soil, but after setting fruit, they can be allowed to dry out between waterings.

Cover the soil with a 3-inch layer of straw mulch to keep the soil cool and conserve moisture. They are strongly structured, requiring no staking.

Fertilizer: Rototill or dig in compost before planting or apply a slow-release fertilizer at planting time. They are not heavy feeders and require no supplemental fertilizer.

◼ *Pest Problems*

There are no pests that I know of. Even the birds leave them alone.

◼ *Harvesting*

Huckleberries are ready to harvest when they turn deep purple to almost black. Wait to pick until the entire cluster is ripe, then the berries will slide easily off the cluster stem, netting a small handful at each pick. Wash them under a gentle stream of water, lay them out to dry, pour onto cookie sheets in a single layer to freeze, then dump them into zip locks to store. Makes wonderful pie when used with other berries, and cut back on the sugar, garden huckleberries are sweet. Good in jams, sauces, and in muffins.

Melons can take up a lot of space in the garden, but they're fun to grow.

MELON Cantaloupe and Watermelon *(Cucumis melo)*

We always find space for a few cantaloupe vines, but just one watermelon vine because they grow quite large. Planting out plant starts, warming up the soil before planting, and selecting short season varieties will give most Rocky Mountain gardeners up to a half dozen cantaloupes per vine and two to three watermelons on one plant. Melons can be greenhouse-grown and grown in 5-gallon or larger containers.

■ *Recommended Varieties*

Melons thrive in hot summer climates. Short-season varieties are essential for success.

Cantaloupe: 'Alvaro' is short season, maturing in 65 days with small fruits, five to six per vine. 'Athena' is one of our favorites, 75-day crop, very sweet, 6-inch fruits with fusarium and powdery mildew resistance. 'Oka' is an heirloom, from Montreal, good for cooler summer climates.
Watermelon: You need 70 days of sunshine and warm soils for watermelon.

'Sugar Baby' is a favorite, 80 days to harvest, small seedless, very sweet, four to six melons per vine. 'New Queen' 80 days, green striped rind and gorgeous orange flesh with very few seeds, 5-pound fruits, high in sugar content. 'Blacktail Mountain', 70 days, developed in northern Idaho for tolerance to cool summer nights, 9-inch fruits on vines that also take the heat.

■ *Planting*

Start melon seeds indoors up to four weeks before planting outside, harden off, and plant one week before the last frost. Plant them in peat pots to transplant without damaging roots. Warm the soil up first by laying out black plastic or woven ground cover cloth a couple of weeks before planting.

Melons need full sun and rich soil full of compost to produce well. Plant seeds in hills at least 4 feet apart, and plant three seeds per hill. Thin plants to one plant every 4 feet after they grow three sets of leaves.

■ *Maintenance*

Water: Melons need deep, slowly applied water about every other day. It is okay to let the soil dry out to 1-inch down between waterings. Use drip irrigation tubing or soaker hoses laid out after planting. Avoid overhead watering to prevent disease.

Fertilizer: Rototill or dig in compost before planting or apply a slow-release fertilizer at planting time.

Pollination: Melon plants have separate male and female flowers on the same plant. The flowers have to be pollinated in order to produce fruits. Plant some pollinating magnets in the area. Cosmos and nasturtiums are good companions to attract pollinators.

■ *Pest Problems*

Melons suffer from the same types of pests that all squash-family plants encounter. Cucumber beetles, flea beetles, squash bugs, and squash vine borers are some of the worst. Use row covers to prevent flying insects from landing on the plants. Lift the row covers for two hours in the morning twice a week to encourage pollination, or hand-pollinate. If you have bad problems with squash bugs and squash vine borers, you might consider growing melons under cover for their entire growing season. Interplant a few radishes among the melon vines and allow them to go to seed. Cucumber beetles are repelled by the radishes and the flowers are a pollinator magnet.

■ *Harvesting*

Melons will be ready to harvest around 30 to 45 days after flowering. Check the stems to look for cracking, with nearby tendrils turning brown and crispy, signs that they are ready. Cantaloupe melons should smell sweet. You may need to sacrifice a melon just to test your instincts. If they aren't ripe, they will be hard inside and the sugar content will be low. Watermelon flesh will be lighter in color and taste flat.

RHUBARB *(Rheum × hybridum)*

Rhubarb stalks can be green or red, depending on the variety you plant.

I remember "helping" Grandma in the garden one early spring morning, still crisp and cool, but the snow was gone. She would grab long stalks that looked like celery at the base, pull and snap them off at the ground. With a quick slice of her kitchen knife, she chopped the giant leaves off and threw them over the fence, cautioning, "Don't touch! They are poisonous!" I asked if I could taste the crunchy things, was given the nod of approval and bit in. She thought my antics hilarious, as I spit the bitter, tart bite on the ground. Upon lugging the filled basket indoors, she quickly diced the rhubarb, threw it into a giant bowl and added many cups of sugar before dumping the sticky clumps into a prepared pie crust. It was like magic. Warm rhubarb pie with a dollop of vanilla ice cream wiped my first not so pleasant memory right away.

■ Recommended Varieties

Rhubarb crowns will be available in your local nursery. You can grow from seed if you start in January, plant out starts in early spring as soon as you can dig. 'Glaskins Perpetual' is an heirloom, available as seed and it likes cool summer regions. 'Crimson Red' is sold as a root division and is very winter hardy. Shipped to plant in late March to the first of April.

■ Planting

Temperature: Rhubarb requires temperatures below 40°F in the winter to break dormancy and temperatures below 75°F to grow well during the summer and replenish its stores for winter growth. Plant in the spring or fall whenever they are available, while the crowns are still dormant. In hot high and low desert regions, afternoon shade is fine.

Soil: Rhubarb grows best in loose, well-drained soil.

Sun: Full sun.

Starting seeds indoors: If you are growing from seed, sow in a greenhouse in January for spring planting.

Planting outside: Cultivate the soil to a depth of 8 to 10 inches. Plant rhubarb crowns 24 inches apart, covering them with just 1 to 2 inches of soil. Water well.

Maintenance

Water: Water rhubarb with the same frequency you'd water sugar snap peas, regularly, but allow to dry out between waterings. Drip irrigation is best.

Fertilizer: Fertilize after harvest with liquid fish emulsion.

Pest Problems

Rhubarb has few pest problems.

Harvesting

Harvest during the third season of growth. A knife can cause crown damage, so grab the stalk with both hands and pull sideways and outward to break the stalk. Never remove more than one-third of the plant at any given time. Stop cutting stalks when they are less than ½ inch wide. Let the plant keep growing to produce reserves to allow it sprout next year. Do not eat the leaves! You can expect 1 to 5 pounds of stalks per plant.

GROWING TIPS

Put your rhubarb in a permanent home since it lives for over twenty years. They make an outstanding landscape plant with their large tropical-looking foliage. At some point during the spring or early summer, your rhubarb plants might begin to flower or "bolt." Cut off this flower stalk as soon as you see it and keep harvesting. Even if the stalk appears after harvest, you still want to cut it off, as leaving it will cause the plant to divert energy to producing seeds, not storing energy in the roots for the next year.

STRAWBERRY *(Fragaria × ananassa)*

We took our regular visits to the strawberry fruit stands dotting the highways and biways of California for granted. There was no need to grow our own with the large, plump, sugary sweet 'Sequoias' available by the case just picked from the fields. Now we have a need for having our own plot of strawberries at the ready, those 'Sequoias' barely resembling the berries we buy at the market after they have been shipped and sitting on the grocer's shelf for days on end. In early summer we pick the sun-ripened fresh berries from plump green plants that have sent out runners to form a dense swath that meanders in and out of the rose bushes. Grown here as a perennial, they like to be moved to a new area every three years or so, to start afresh from their self-produced long runners. They can also be grown as an annual, as commercial growers do, planted in spring from starts and giving you fruit by summer's end.

Use nets to ensure you'll get to eat your strawberries before the birds do.

■ *Recommended Varieties*

There are June-bearing, everbearing, and day-neutral strawberries. As with many fruit crops, it is best to purchase plants from local growers.

Because of the number of diseases that affect strawberries, buy resistant varieties when possible.

June-bearing: 'All-Star', 'Guardian', 'Lateglow', 'Tioga', 'Totem', 'Puget Reliance', 'Ranier'
Everbearing: 'Fort Laramie', 'Ozark Beauty', 'Quinault'
Day neutral: 'Tribute', 'Tristar'

■ *Planting*

Plant bare-root strawberry plants each spring. Plant container-grown plants in early spring. Strawberries grow best in full sun in well-drained soils.

To grow plants as perennials, plant strawberries 2 feet apart with 4 feet between rows. Allow runners to fill in the row to create a 2-foot mat with a final spacing of 2 feet between rows.

You can plant new strawberries in spring and allow them to send out runners throughout summer that will bloom and fruit the following year. You can also transplant larger plants in fall and allow them to produce fruits in spring.

If anthracnose is a problem, dig up plants after harvesting, and plant new plants each fall in a new area.

■ *Maintenance*

Water: Strawberries require regular, deep watering to a depth of 6 to 8 inches throughout the growing season, but you can stop watering during the winter months.

Mulch: All strawberries do best when mulched to conserve moisture, keep weeds under control, and keep the berries from touching the soil.

Fertilizer: Apply slow-release fertilizer at planting time or in spring and again in early summer. Watch for iron deficiencies and treat accordingly with applications of chelated iron.

■ *Pest Problems*

Use nets to keep the birds from eating the fruits as they ripen. Multiple fungal and bacterial problems attack strawberry plants. If you think your plants could be afflicted, the best thing to do is to dig up a plant and take it to your local Cooperative Extension office for help with diagnosis and treatment solutions.

■ *Harvesting*

The plants will flower and fruit in mid- to late-summer. Harvest when the fruits are colorful and can be easily pulled off the plant.

CHAPTER 7

VEGETABLE & HERB GARDENING

There is no doubt that homegrown tomatoes far surpass the ones you buy at the market in taste, texture, sweetness, and acidity. There is so much difference, it's almost like they were two different fruits. Where I live, most of the freshest produce comes from growing your own or from the farmers market. Most produce in the supermarkets is trucked in. The farther away from the source, the longer the produce has sat in trucks. It could very well have been harvested a week before being loaded and shipped. If you can grow even a little bit of your own edibles, like a potted rosemary or tomato plant, you can enjoy homegrown fruits and veggies, with very little time, space, or effort.

Vegetable Gardening Throughout the Year

In the Rocky Mountain region, there is a cooler time of the year (cool season) and a warmer time of the year (warm season) for gardening. Where they fall in the calendar and how long they last depends on where you live. Different plants grow during warm and cool seasons. The key to successful vegetable gardening is planting the right plant, in the right place, and at the right time of year.

In higher elevations of the Rocky Mountain states, vegetables thought of as "cool season" will grow on through the warm summer season, and if picked frequently, may very well keep on producing to the cool of fall until the first frost. Swiss chard, broccoli, lettuce, and carrots grow throughout the summer in these regions. In these same areas, the key to planting warm-weather veggies lies in getting a head start by either growing or buying the plants in pots, then planting them when the soil has warmed up after danger of last frost is passed. At the end of their growing cycle, when they are producing fruits for harvest, they may need our assistance in helping them complete their goal.

In the low and high desert regions, cool-season vegetables will grow from April to June and August to October. In these areas, cool spring weather can seemingly disappear in just a couple of weeks time, leading directly into high summer temps, causing cool-season crops to bolt. Planting hardier transplants before the last frost date and providing frost protection for a few weeks gets them on their way to producing quickly, before the heat rises. The warm-season veggies and herbs thrive in these hot summer regions, although they may still need a jumpstart in spring by planting out transplants, pre-warming the soil, and providing frost protection for common late season frosts.

To find out when to start seeds for growing transplants and when to direct sow cool- and warm-season crops, see the individual plant profiles. Here are two simple tips to plant at the right time.

- Plant warm-season vegetables when the soil temperature is at least 60°F (65°F to 70°F is even better!).
- Plant cool-season vegetables in the spring when soil temperatures are at least 45°F, and the ground has thawed. Plant the vegetables for a fall harvest by seed in August in all areas or plant transplants when nighttime air temperatures are regularly below 60°F.

The vegetable and herb profiles in this book are organized to help you distinguish cool- and warm-season vegetables so there is no question as to what you should be planting when. Some perennial types make easy choices if they are cold hardy to your zone. Once you plant perennials and get them established, you need not pay them much attention in subsequent seasons.

Transitioning between Warm- and Cool-Season Gardening

It's easier to transition a vegetable garden between seasons if crops are planted in rows or blocks. Designed this way, you can easily save part of the garden for the next season crops, or you can pull up all of one crop and plant another.

Raised beds and small-space gardens can be more challenging. You have to find ways to shoehorn in the new crop while the old crop is finishing up. If you plant a crop in different parts of the garden for diversity, or intercrop with other crops to save space, then you can end up with small spaces to fill all over the garden. Ideally, you want to be ready to plant a new crop when you have pulled the last one.

A little bit of planning goes a long way when making the transition. In Chapter 4, we discuss the steps in planning the garden, which includes drawing the garden plan to scale. Winter is a good time to sit down with the previous years' garden plan to refresh your memory. Some crops, like broccoli, need to be rotated to a new bed each year. A garden map makes the job easier to find a new spot to move them to and in assigning other crops to their spaces. With a colored pencil, write in the cool-season plants you plan to grow, those will come first. In a different-colored pencil, write in the warm-season plants that will fill the spots when the cool-season vegetables are finished. Don't forget to pencil in the companion plants at the same time. This small bit of organization helps to figure out the quantities of plants you need to grow or to buy. Keep each garden plot plan (make sure you title it by the year) for future garden planning.

Small-Space Vegetable Gardening

Don't say no to edibles, even if you have only a small amount of space in the sun. Raised-bed kits, self-watering containers, and vertical-gardening assemblies allow you to grow vegetables anywhere, with any amount of space. Growing in raised beds or containers lets you more easily control the quality of the soil. Incorporating edibles into the existing landscape utilizes the space, and more importantly, gives homeowners, and apartment and condominium dwellers, the opportunity to grow their own fruits and vegetables.

Find Your Favorite Vegetables and Herbs

Ready to get growing? Use this mini-index to find the edibles you want to learn about.

(cs denotes cool season)
(ws denotes warm season)

You can see the rows of newly planted seeds delineated by the lighter-colored seed-starting mix covering the seeds.

Cool-Season Gardening Tips & Tricks

The cool season of vegetable gardening can begin in late winter in milder valley climates, but run through the cooler summer in higher elevation areas. Some hardier plants, planted in fall, can be harvested through spring. Others require successive plantings in order to get a continuous harvest. This is noted in individual plant descriptions where applicable.

Scheduling can be confusing. Cool-season crops sprout from seed when soil temperatures are relatively high (75°F to 85°F), but do their best growing when air temperatures start to cool down. Broccoli, cabbage, kale, and many other members of the cabbage family are like this. You will sow these plants outside in late summer, but they will grow and mature during the cooler fall season. If you grow these plants from transplants, you can also plant cool-season crops early in spring to take advantage of cool weather. However, most will bolt or stop producing when the weather is too warm.

Planting Seeds Outside

Many of the cool-season vegetables are easy to grow from seeds planted directly into the garden. This is indicated in the individual plant profiles.

Follow the instructions on the seed packets and in the plant profiles regarding the planting depth. Some seeds, such as peas, need to be planted fairly deep, while others, such as lettuce, barely need to be covered. A good rule of thumb is to sow seed twice as deep as the seed is wide. Very fine seed is sprinkled on the surface of the soil and lightly covered with sand or seed mix. Larger seeds, like pumpkin, are planted 1 inch deep.

Use seed-starting mix instead of regular garden soil. This lightweight mix makes it easy for sprouting seedlings to break out above the soil.

Keep seeds moist while they are sprouting. Some established plants can deal with a bit of drought or water fluctuations, but seeds must stay evenly moist while sprouting.

Planting Transplants

Some plants are much easier to grow from transplants. Some may need to be started indoors from February through April in order to grow them to a larger size before planting them out.

Always harden off transplants before planting outside—even if you bought them at a garden center. Hardening off is the process of getting plants used to outdoor conditions, including sun, temperature, and wind. By gradually exposing them to higher light levels, light breezes, and warmer temperatures, the plants toughen up to the elements, minimizing transplant shock. This preliminary hardening-off process starts the plants growing as soon as they are put into the garden soil.

Steps to Harden off Transplants

- Start by putting your transplants in sheltered, semi-shady location for about two weeks, moving them back indoors at night.
- Then move them to a sunnier location for another week, but if frost threatens, bring them back indoors.
- When all danger of frost is passed, move them to the spot where they will grow, but leave them in the pots for few days to acclimate them.
- Be sure to give them extra water during the hardening off process. They will dry out more quickly outdoors. Then, plant in the garden bed.
- Plant transplants at the recommended finished spacing for the mature plants to eliminate thinning.

Planning for a Continual Harvest

Succession planting is the process of planting the same plant, several weeks apart, several times throughout the growing season. Lettuce, carrots, radishes, and turnips are examples of plants that you can plant in succession. By planting several crops of these vegetables on a staggered schedule, you ensure a bountiful harvest of produce throughout the growing season. Sow seeds for successive crops between the rows of the existing plants. If a vegetable is a good candidate for succession planting, this is indicated in the plant profile.

Harvesting

In warmer areas of the Rocky Mountain states you can plant some vegetables, like carrots, in the fall and harvest through early winter with minimal protection. The garden bed acts as a sort of "cold storage," as a damp surrounding soil looses heat more slowly. In some lower valley and desert regions, crops can be overwintered under a thick bed of straw for harvesting in early spring.

Other vegetables can be harvested at any point during their growth cycle. Turnips and beets, for example, taste just as good when harvested at 1 inch in diameter as they do when harvested at 3 inches. You can't leave them in the ground, but by planting successive rounds of seeds, you can harvest all season, at various stages of the growth cycle.

Still other plants have to be harvested when they're ready—there's no early harvesting or "cold storage." Cabbage, broccoli, and cauliflower should be harvested as heads and crowns form. Broccoli and cauliflower are easy to freeze and will keep for six to eight months.

Over time, you will get the hang of which vegetables can stay in the garden until you're ready for them, which ones can be eaten early, and which ones you need to harvest at a specific point in the growth cycle.

Cover Cropping

If you have spaces during the growing season, or after the warm-season crops are finished, consider cover cropping. This is the practice of planting a nitrogen-fixing legume such as winter rye, cereal rye, clover, fava beans, or peas in an unused section of the garden. Let these plants grow until they are about to flower. Then, cut them down and turn them under into the soil as a "green manure." Cover cropping is an inexpensive way to add nutrients to the soil while preventing erosion from wind or water during winter.

Crop Rotation

Certain plants in the cool-season vegetable garden are highly susceptible to soil-borne diseases. Changing where you plant from season to season helps avoid those problems. Cabbage-family plants, including broccoli, cauliflower, collards, kale, and cabbage, have problems with soil diseases and fungi. If you find yourself facing continual soil-borne diseases, consider growing just those crops in containers with new soil each season.

ARUGULA *(Eruca vesicaria)*

Across from my produce stand, another participating farmer had set up her tables laden with beautiful radishes, beets, and mounds of crisp arugula. Every time a customer loaded up a bag, their pungent aroma was released, drawing in herds of shoppers by their scent. Arugula is an annual green that thrives during cool weather. It needs 45 to 60 days to mature. In regions with short growing seasons, start seeds earlier to bring to harvest before snowfall. For the early spring crop, you can germinate then grow starts of arugula in winter, aided by a hoop house or tunnel for protection. Arugula is hardy to temperatures around 20°F, so have some frost cloth handy if the forecast is for colder weather in your area. Summer-grown arugula has a wasabi-hot flavor—different than the milder winter greens. Once the plants start to bolt (send up flower stalks), they're nearing the end of their life cycle. You can cut off the stalks to prolong leaf production and the flowers are edible, but eventually it's better to move on to harvesting from newer plantings.

Recommended Varieties

The straight species of salad arugula grows fine in all regions. The salad arugula variety 'Astro' is heat-tolerant, a plus if you plan to grow arugula through the summer in warmer regions. 'Astro II' matures earlier (35 days) and is a good choice for colder climates. Wild arugula (*Diplotaxis tenuifolia*) is a type of arugula with longer, more deeply incised (cut) leaves. It is spicier than salad arugula. A couple of other good choices are 'Sylvetta' and 'Gladiator'.

When and Where to Plant

Temperature: Arugula grows best in cool weather. Direct sow four weeks before last frost or six weeks before first frost. In regions with hot summers, grow arugula in partial shade and provide ample water to grow the crop throughout the season.

Soil: Plants thrive in deep, fertile soil with lots of organic matter. Arugula grows fine in our alkaline soils.

Sun: Full sun to partial shade.

How to Plant

Starting seeds indoors: You can start seeds indoors four weeks before planting out. You do not need a heat mat, as arugula prefers cooler temperatures.

Planting outside: Soak the seeds overnight before planting outside for faster germination.

GROWING TIPS

For milder leaves in summer, provide arugula plants with some shade.

To keep pests away from arugula, plant away from cabbage-family plants (which harbor the same pests).

How to Grow

Water: Arugula needs steady moisture, particularly as the weather warms, to keep it from bolting.

Fertilizer: Sidedress with a balanced fertilizer (10-10-10, for example) once a month to encourage steady leaf production, or apply a slow-release fertilizer at planting time.

Pest control: Flea beetles are the most common pests to strike arugula. Use floating row covers to control these pests when they are active.

When and How to Harvest

Arugula is cut and come again. Young leaves are tender and mild, while older leaves are spicier and better for braising. Use scissors to cut the leaves at the base of the plant. Do not pull up the entire plant.

Mix arugula in with other salad greens.

ASPARAGUS *(Asparagus officinalis)*

Asparagus is a long-lived perennial vegetable that can command a high price at the market in off season. It's best to grow and harvest it yourself if you have the space. The most difficult aspect of growing asparagus for most gardeners is patience. You have to wait at least three years from the time you plant to when you harvest. It's worth the wait, though, if you have an area where you can plant asparagus crowns and leave them alone to grow. Because the crop isn't ready for harvest all at once, pick as the spears are ready, save them in the refrigerator (if you can!), then blanch and freeze. Frozen spears are just as tasty as fresh!

◼ *Recommended Varieties*

Plant all-male varieties of 'Jersey Giant', 'Jersey Prince', or 'Jersey Knight'. 'Millennium' is cold tolerant and 'Mary Washington' is a popular heirloom. Buy asparagus crowns from a local resource. They will be one-year-old plants that should produce the third season after planting.

◼ *When and Where to Plant*

Temperature: Plant asparagus crowns when the soil has warmed to a temperature of at least 50°F in early spring. If planted when the soil is any cooler, the plants can succumb to crown rot.

Soil: Asparagus plants grow best in a loose, well-drained soil and in our alkaline soil conditions.

Sun: Full sun.

◼ *How to Plant*

Starting seeds indoors: Not recommended.

Planting outside: Dig a furrow or trench that is 6 inches deep. Place the crowns 12 inches apart in the furrow and then cover with 2 to 3 inches of soil and water. When plants are 4-inches tall,

It takes a few years before you can harvest asparagus, but the results are worth the wait.

sidedress with a fertilizer high in nitrogen, then cover again with a few inches of soil. Repeat every few weeks until furrow is filled. Space rows 1 to 2 feet apart.

How to Grow

Water: Asparagus plants are fairly drought-tolerant, but they will need to be watered with about the same frequency that you would water a new tree or shrub (once or twice a week) while they're getting established. After the first season, water once a week if your area sees no measurable precipitation. Do not overwater! The roots of the plant don't like to sit in wet soil!

Fertilizer: Watch for iron deficiencies and apply chelated iron per package instructions. Fertilize plants with composted chicken manure or compost at the end of the harvest season (mid-summer to early fall) to encourage good growth and storage for the next year's harvest.

Pest control: Asparagus has few pest problems.

How to Harvest

Harvest during the third season of growth (after the plant is two years old). The asparagus shoots will start to emerge once the soil warms up to about 50°F. Harvest 6-inch spears by snapping them off at the base of the soil. Harvest two to four times a week. Once the spears start to be less than $\frac{3}{8}$ inch in diameter, stop harvesting and let the spears grow into ferns. This growth will photosynthesize and produce energy for the next year.

GROWING TIPS

Cultivate lightly around asparagus plants during the first year to reduce weed problems. Straw mulch is also useful when growing asparagus.

Let the tops of the plants grow throughout the summer. Do not cut back the tops until the following spring when you see new shoots.

BEET *(Beta vulgaris)*

Beets are thought of as sweet, red round roots that are most often pickled or used for color in soups. Thankfully, they have risen above their stereotype to find their way to the table in a myriad of forms. Their juvenile leaves can be used in salads; the mature leaves are prepared in similar ways as spinach—blanched, steamed, stir fried, sautéed, and stewed. Beet roots are still pickled, but the sweetness is enhanced when roasted or grilled. Beets are available in tried-and-true heirloom varieties and in hybrid forms with disease-resistance and cold-tolerance for overwintering. They come in all hues of red, striped, white, and even golden yellow tones. Beets need full sun and loose soil to form good roots. Greens are ready for harvest within a few weeks and beet roots can be dug in 45 to 50 days from direct sown seed.

■ *Recommended Varieties*

The following red varieties grow well in the Rocky Mountain regions: 'Ruby Queen', 'Early Wonder Tall Top', 'Red Ace', 'Pacemaker II', and 'Detroit Dark Red'. Heirlooms varieties include: 'Yellow Mangel', which is yellow, and 'Chioggia', which has red-and-white-stripes.

■ *When and Where to Plant*

Temperature: Beets germinate best when soil temperatures are 55°F to 75°F. The plants grow best when air temperatures are 60°F to 65°F. Direct-sow seeds four weeks before the last frost with successive sowing every two to three weeks in regions with cooler summers to eight to ten weeks before the first frost. Beets can overwinter in USDA Zones 5 and up with a thick cover of straw mulch.

Soil: Beets need deep, loose, fertile soils and grow fine in our alkaline soils.

Sun: Full sun.

GROWING TIPS

Beets are an easy crop to grow, even in container gardens. Plant a large (15-gallon capacity or more) container with lettuce greens and scallions for a salad bowl garden. In the garden, they make good companions with kohlrabi, bush beans, and members of the cabbage family. Beets planted at the proper time have fewer pest problems than beets planted late. If you're confused about when to plant, err on the side of earlier.

Newer hybrid varieties are sweeter than older varieties.

■ *How to Plant*

Starting seeds indoors: Not recommended.

Planting outside: Sow seeds outside 2 inches apart and ½ inch deep. Thin to 4 inches apart when they reach 6 inches tall.

■ *How to Grow*

Water: Beets need even moisture to avoid scab, a condition in which brown, raised patches form on the outsides of the roots.

Fertilizer: Use a balanced fertilizer when planting. Apply phosphorus if a soil test indicates it is needed.

Pest control: Cercospora leaf spot is a fungus that causes brown scabby spots on leaves and interferes with sugar production and root development. Plant resistant varieties.

■ *When and How to Harvest*

To harvest juvenile beet greens for salads while keeping the roots growing, use scissors to cut no more than one-quarter of the leaves at any time or use the thinnings. To check if roots are ready to harvest, pull one up as a test. Beets are at their finest when harvested small, 3 to 4 inches in diameter.

Both the tops and the roots of beets can be eaten.

BROCCOLI *(Brassica oleracea,* Italica Group*)*

Like all vegetables in the cabbage family, broccoli is highly nutritious, carrying over ten vitamins and being very high in fiber. Broccoli thrives in the cooler Rocky Mountain regions from late spring through the summer, but is best grown as a very early spring or as a fall crop in areas with hot summers. Rotate where you plant broccoli in the garden from year to year to prevent plants from succumbing to soil-borne diseases. Broccoli freezes well, maintaining its flavor and texture.

■ *Recommended Varieties*

'Umpqua', 'Packman', and 'Belstar' are ready in 60 to 66 days; 'Apollo' produces many side shoots.

■ *When and Where to Plant*

Temperature: Broccoli germinates best when soil temperatures are 50°F to 75°F. It is best to use transplants in our region for early spring plantings. In colder winter areas, start seeds indoors six to eight weeks before transplanting outdoors six to eight weeks before the last frost. For a fall crop, direct sow fourteen weeks before the first frost or use transplants planted in the garden eight weeks before the first frost.

Soil: Broccoli grows well in our Rocky Mountain soils.

Sun: Full sun.

■ *How to Plant*

Starting seeds indoors: Start seeds indoors at least 40 days before you want to plant transplants outside. Broccoli takes 3 to 10 days to germinate and about a month to grow to transplant size.

Planting outside: Always harden off your transplants before planting them outside in spring. Leave 12 to 18 inches between transplants.

Successive crops of broccoli can be grown throughout the cool season.

GROWING TIPS

Don't compost broccoli plants—doing so can spread the myriad diseases affecting them to your entire compost pile.

Some varieties of broccoli are extremely temperature sensitive. If there's a cold snap (temperatures of 35°F to 50°F) for more than ten days after broccoli is planted, the plants will bolt (flower), and you won't get a head to harvest. You can try to prevent the cold from affecting the plants by covering them with a cold frame or floating row covers. Once the plants bolt, you have to just pull them up and start over.

How to Grow

Water: Keep broccoli evenly moist throughout the growing season.

Fertilizer: Add compost to the soil before planting.

Pest control: Broccoli and other cabbage-family plants are susceptible to a variety of pests, including aphids, cabbage whites, cabbage loopers, diamondback moths, flea beetles, harlequin bugs, and slugs. Plant resistant varieties when possible and use floating row covers when flying insects are active. Use Neem oil and *Bacillus thuringiensis* (*B.t.*) to control a wide range of pests.

When and How to Harvest

Cut the center flowerhead when it is still dark green and tight (about 60 days for most varieties—it will say on the seed packet). When the head starts to loosen and turn yellow, it's too late to harvest. If you're growing a variety that produces side shoots, leave the rest of the plant in the garden for up to two months. Provide mulch and shade cloth to keep from bolting in the heat. If the variety is primarily grown for the large center head, cut the heads and pull up the rest of the plant to make room for other vegetable crops.

BRUSSELS SPROUTS
(*Brassica oleracea,* Gemmifera Group)

Brussels sprouts, no longer relegated to the table as a steamed veggie, really strut their rich flavors when roasted or even skewered and grilled. One reason to grow this unusual-looking cabbage-family plant is that it likes cooler climates, even sweetening up with some frost. It is easy to grow if you can keep the pests away and are patient. Most types need 80 to 100 days from seed to harvest.

The "sprouts" of Brussels sprouts develop along the plant stem. You harvest from the bottom up.

■ *Recommended Varieties*

'Franklin' is a taller variety that produces earlier sprouts in 80 days. 'Roodnerf' hybrids are medium to tall plants that are quite cold hardy. 'Catskill' and 'Rubine' are heirlooms. 'Catskill' is a dwarf variety that needs 100 days to mature. 'Rubine' has beautiful purple-red sprouts.

■ *When and Where to Plant*

Temperature: Brussels sprouts can start growing in the warmer days of mid-summer, but will need cool weather in order to mature. In cool summer regions, sow seed six to eight weeks before planting hardened-off transplants outdoors six weeks before the last frost. In warm summer zones, sow seed for transplants six to eight weeks before planting in the garden four to six weeks before the first frost.

Soil: Add compost to the soil before planting. Brussels sprouts are heavy feeders. Brussels sprouts enjoy alkaline soils with higher pH levels to help keep soil-borne diseases at bay.

Sun: Full sun.

How to Plant

Starting seeds indoors: It takes 30 to 45 days to grow plants for transplanting outside. You'll need to harden off the plants before planting outside—the plants need to get used to the late summer heat before they go in the garden.

Planting outside: Plant transplants in the garden 16 to 18 inches apart.

How to Grow

Water: Keep evenly moist throughout the growing season.

Fertilizer: Fertilize with a balanced fertilizer once a month throughout the growing season.

Pest control: Cutworms can affect transplants. To protect young plants, loosely wrap the bottom 3 to 4 inches of stem with newspaper or foil. Cabbageworms can attack larger plant leaves. If you see evidence of cabbageworms, control with *Bacillus thuringiensis* (*B.t.*). Growing Brussels sprouts as a fall crop helps control aphids, as they don't like cooler temps.

When and How to Harvest

Wait to harvest Brussels sprouts until they've been hit by several frosts. They'll be much sweeter. You can start harvesting the sprouts about two months after planting. The sprouts will mature from the bottom up. As a sprout begins to form, clip off the leaf below the sprout and let it grow to be ¾ to 1 inch in diameter. Then use clippers to harvest the sprouts as they mature. (You can take enough at a time to eat!)

GROWING TIPS

Brussels sprouts can be grown in container gardens in pots that are at least 12 inches deep. Brussels sprouts are shallow rooted and prone to falling over. Stake the taller varieties to keep these plants upright and away from the soil.

CABBAGE *(Brassica oleracea)*

Cabbage is a classic cool-season vegetable. It is best suited for cooler summer climes, but warmer regions can grow early varieties if transplants are started indoors. You can't beat it for utility—it is easy to store and can be added to soups, stir-fries, and cold salads. Along with other cruciferous vegetables, cabbage is one of the most nutritious vegetables you can eat.

■ *Recommended Varieties*

'Danish Ballhead', 'Excel', 'Gloria', 'Melissa', and 'Zerlina' are all resistant to common cabbage diseases such as fusarium wilt, yellows, and black rot. Select cabbage varieties with shortest days to harvest. 'Quickstart' is ready in just 55 days; 'Derby Day' in 58 days; 'Parel' is early maturing at 50 days.

■ *When and Where to Plant*

Temperature: Cabbage needs soil temperatures of at least 50°F to germinate and air temperatures of 60°F to 65°F. Temperature fluctuations can cause spring plantings to bolt. Plant transplants outside as soon as the ground can be worked, two to four weeks before the last frost. For a fall crop, start seed in a cool location in June, transplant to the garden in August. Most are ready for harvest 60 days after planting.

Soil: Cabbage grows best in well-drained, fertile soil. Add compost before planting. Higher-pH alkaline soils such as ours keep club-root disease at bay.

Sun: Full sun.

GROWING TIP

Rotate the cabbage planting areas in your garden, never replanting in the same place more frequently than every two years. Cabbage plants and other cruciferous vegetables are highly susceptible to diseases that linger in the soil. If you have limited space and plan to grow just a few heads per year, consider making a "cabbage barrel" in which you can replace the soil each time you plant new cabbages. Plant thyme with cabbages to help repel the cabbage butterfly.

Cabbage is easy to grow and easy to store.

How to Plant

Starting seeds indoors: Sow seeds indoors six to eight weeks before the last frost or before planting out in mid-summer for a fall crop. Harden off transplants before planting outdoors in spring.

Planting outside: Because smaller cabbage heads taste better and store more easily, plant cabbage transplants 12 to 18 inches apart in rows 3 feet apart or on 24-inch centers if growing in raised beds. The plants will grow to be 12 to 24 inches in diameter.

How to Grow

Water: Cabbages need evenly moist soil throughout their growing period. Once the heads start to firm up, you can keep the soil on the drier side.

Fertilizer: Sidedress with organic, slow-release fertilizer at the time of planting. One month after planting, apply another application.

Pest control: Look for caterpillars eating the leaves. (They're most likely to show up in fall and spring—not winter.) If you see them, treat with *Bacillus thuringiensis* (*B.t.*) to control them.

When and How to Harvest

The part of the cabbage that you harvest is called a head, and smaller heads taste better. Once the head feels firm, it is ready to pick. Use pruners or a knife to cut off the head just below the base. Leave the stem in the ground because you might get a few smaller heads to form. Pick them when ripe.

CARROT *(Daucus carota* ssp. *sativus)*

My earliest childhood garden memories are of carrots. My dad would take me out to the side of the garage in the middle of winter, shovel in hand, to dig through the snow down to the layers of burlap that were peeled back to a final thick covering of straw. The anticipation built as I piled the straw up to reveal the greenish yellow tops of the treasure below. He would plunge in the digging fork, then pry up thick, orange, crisp, covered in soil and wriggling with worms—carrots. Everyone who gardens in the Rocky Mountain region can have carrots on their table throughout the year. They are easy to grow, harvest, store, and preserve.

■ *Recommended Varieties*

For the traditional carrot, grow 'Danvers Half Long', 'Spartan Bonus', 'Scarlet Nantes', 'Nevis' (heat tolerant), 'Apache', 'Camden', or 'Chantenay'. 'Orlando Gold' is a yellow variety. 'Thumbelina' carrots grow fat and round and 'Little Finger' carrots are true "baby carrots," growing to 4 inches or less. Both are good for containers. 'Merida' is an overwinter carrot. Plant late September, overwinter under thick layers of straw, and harvest May through June. It is heat tolerant.

For best results, plant carrots in soil that is loose and free of rocks.

■ *When and Where to Plant*

Temperature: Carrots will germinate when the soil temperature is 45°F to 85°F. They'll grow best at temperatures of 60°F to 65°F. They can stay in the garden all winter in USDA Zones 6 and above without cover and in the garden all summer in other zones. Sow seeds outdoors four weeks before the last frost with successive plantings every three weeks until ten weeks before the projected first frost.

Soil: The most important part of growing carrots is the soil. Turn the soil and work finely sifted compost into it before planting. For carrots to grow long, even roots, the soil has to be loose and free of rocks. Raised beds work well and you can even grow carrots in containers. If you have rocky shallow soils, try varieties that are small, shorter, and round in shape.

Sun: Full sun to partial shade.

■ *How to Plant*

Starting seeds indoors: Not recommended.

Planting outside: Cover seeds with seed-starting mix, and keep the seeds moist while germinating, from six days up to three weeks. Apply water in a mist a couple of times a day if necessary.

■ *How to Grow*

Water: Keep moist while germinating and evenly watered during the growing season.

Thinning: Thin carrots to 3 inches apart when they start crowding each other, at about 4 inches tall. Be ruthless and you will only have to thin once! Use the thinings in salad.

Fertilizer: Add compost to the garden before planting.

Pest control: Carrot rust fly can be a problem. You usually won't know if you have the pest until you harvest and you see their tunneling system throughout the carrots. If you have reports of them in your area, use preventative measures using row crop covers and crop rotation. Also try interplanting with basil, onions, leek, rosemary, or sage. The critters don't like those companions.

■ *When and How to Harvest*

Carrots take 55 to 75 days to grow to maturity. You can harvest them as soon as the roots turn orange (or red, white, purple, or yellow, depending on the variety). Don't let any carrots grow to be larger than 1½ inches wide—they'll start to taste like turpentine at that point. To harvest, just grasp the leafy top and pull or in heavy soils, use a hand digging trowel or fork. You don't have to harvest every carrot at the same time, digging what you need at the time. Or harvest them all and preserve by canning, drying, or freezing.

GROWING TIPS

Mix carrot seeds with fine sand to make sowing the seeds easier. Sowing too thickly makes for tedious thinning. You can also purchase carrot seed tape, which eliminates any thinning on your part. Cover the orange tops of the carrot roots if they start to peek out. Exposure to light will make them turn green or brown. Too much nitrogen fertilizer will make carrots grow large tops and small roots. Carrots don't compete well with weeds, so make sure to pull weeds from around carrots as soon as you see them. In hot summer areas, apply straw mulch.

CAULIFLOWER *(Brassica oleracea,* Botrytis Group*)*

Cauliflower is easiest to grow for gardeners in cool summer regions. It is very picky about air temps. One day of 85°F can cause the heads to toughen and harden. Just like us, they love cool springtime weather when they can languish in the full sun without getting too warm, and they thrive in the early fall when the sun sits low and warm, but it still isn't frosty at night. There are types with typical creamy white heads and also non-traditional hues of chartreuse, purple, and even orange cauliflower available.

To get white heads on your cauliflower, tie the top of the leaves together over the first small curds.

■ *Recommended Varieties*

'Amazing' takes 68 days to maturity and is both heat and cold tolerant. It grows well in the fall. 'Snow Crown' is a fast grower (50 days to maturity) that also tolerates swings in the weather. 'Fremont' is self-blanching and does not require tying. 'Green Macerata' is an heirloom with chartreuse heads.

GROWING TIPS

To get pretty white cauliflower heads, you have to blanch them. Blanching prevents light from reaching the heads, which prevents them from coloring up, hence the term *blanching*, which also means whitening. When the small cauliflower curds begin to form (they will look like baby cauliflowers), use twine to tie the top leaves of the plants together.

Cauliflowers are temperature sensitive. If a cold snap is predicted (temperatures under 50°F for more than ten days in a row), cover the plants with frost cloth, row covers, or poly (rolls of clear plastic) to keep the temperature steady. Otherwise, the plants will bolt.

◼ *When and Where to Plant*

Temperature: Cauliflower is more sensitive to day/night temperature swings than other plants. In fact, for best growth, daytime temperatures should be 60°F to 70°F and nighttime temperatures 50°F to 60°F. Plant hardened-off cauliflower transplants outside after all danger of frost has passed for early spring harvest. Plant transplants outdoors eight weeks before the first frost for fall harvest.

Soil: Cauliflower will do fine in our soils, but they are heavy feeders, so incorporate compost to the garden before planting.

Sun: Full sun.

◼ *How to Plant*

Starting seeds indoors: Start seeds indoors eight to twelve weeks before planting outside. Seeds germinate with soil temperatures of 45°F to 85°F.

Planting outside: Space transplants 15 to 18 inches apart and plant them 2 to 3 inches deeper than the soil line. The stems will elongate as the plants grow.

◼ *How to Grow*

Water: Keep plants evenly moist throughout the growing season. If plants become stressed because of drought or dry soil, they will button and you'll lose the heads.

Fertilizer: Cauliflower is a heavy feeder—particularly of nitrogen and potassium. Sidedress with a balanced fertilizer once a month during the growing season, or apply a slow-release fertilizer at planting time.

Pest control: Cauliflower plants are susceptible to the same pests and diseases that afflict all cabbage-family plants. Protect young plants from cutworms by wrapping their stems with newspaper. Cabbage loopers and cabbageworms attack cauliflower—though less in fall. Keep an eye out for worms. If you see them, you can use *Bacillus thuringiensis* (*B.t.*) as an organic remedy. Interplant cauliflower with thyme, celery, sage, or onions. The pests don't care for these companions.

◼ *When and How to Harvest*

Check the seed packet or plant tag to determine when your cauliflower plants will be ready for harvest (the number of days from planting to maturity). Once they're ready, pull up the entire plant. Cauliflower heads cannot sit in the garden once they've reached maturity—they'll start to have problems with rot and fungus, and they may bolt. They do, however, have a long storage life. Store dry heads in the refrigerator for three weeks. Blanch and freeze portions of the heads for up to a year.

COLLARDS *(Brassica oleracea,* Acephala Group*)*

Collards are commonly found in gardens and kitchens in the southern states, but they have found their way to tables across the country. Collards are cholesterol lowering and an antioxidant, high in vitamins K, A, C, manganese, and iron. They grow well in all of the Rocky Mountain regions, and are extremely cold hardy, not minding at all if temperatures dip to 10°F. They are a great crop to grow in winter under hoops and tunnels with frost and snow protection. Throw a good-sized handful of chopped collards into the soup pot at the end of the cooking cycle to maintain the structure and the vitamins. Sauté, stir fry, or steam, but don't overcook. You will keep all that goodness but avoid the smell associated with collards that are overdone.

■ *Recommended Varieties*

The best varieties for the Rocky Mountain regions include 'Flash' and 'Champion', slow to bolt and ready to harvest in 55 days. 'Vates' collards is an heirloom dwarf, and heat-resistant.

■ *When and Where to Plant*

Temperature: Seeds will germinate in temperatures of 50°F to 85°F. Direct-sow outside 4 weeks before the last frost, with repeat sowings every two weeks until two weeks after the last frost. For a fall/winter crop, sow seeds eight to ten weeks before the first frost.

Soil: For the biggest plants, add generous amounts of compost or composted manure to the garden before planting collards.

Sun: Full sun to partial shade.

GROWING TIPS

As a leafy green, collards are heavy feeders and need a steady supply of nitrogen to keep growing. Sidedress with a high-nitrogen fertilizer every four weeks during the growing season. Composted chicken manure works well for this.

Rotate the planting area for collards and other cabbage-family plants, and try not to plant in the same place more frequently than every three years.

If you direct-sow collards into the garden, you'll have to thin some of the seedlings. Don't throw out these young plants! Add them to salads or stir-fries. Smaller collard leaves aren't stringy.

How to Plant

Starting seeds indoors: Direct sown seeds are best.
Planting outside: Sow seeds 2 inches apart. When plants are 4 to 6 inches tall, thin plants to 12 to 24 inches apart.

How to Grow

Water: Keep plants evenly moist, never allowing the soil to completely dry out.
Fertilizer: Fertilize every four weeks during the growing season. Mulch with grass clippings and other high-nitrogen materials to encourage steady leaf growth.
Pest control: Use floating row covers to cover collard plants when you see white butterflies (cabbagewhites) around the plants. If you see cabbageworms, you can use *Bacillus thuringiensis* (*B.t.*) to control them.

When and How to Harvest

Harvest individual leaves and allow the plant to keep growing throughout the season. Start by cutting the outermost leaves first, which will keep the plant growing. Once the plant has matured (in 50 to 70 days), you can also cut the entire plant and bring it inside to process. Collards will keep in the refrigerator crisper drawer for a few weeks, but they taste better and have more nutrients when they're eaten soon after harvesting.

Opposite: Collards are easy to grow and good for you!

Once harvested, garlic can be stored in a cool, dry location.

GARLIC *(Allium sativum)*

You can never have too much garlic. Our first fall gardening season, I planted fifty garlic bulbs (seed), rationalizing that one head a week should do it. After harvesting in July, I was out of garlic by summers' end. Now I plant hundreds of cloves spaced just inches apart in a designated garlic garden, with the goal of having enough garlic to last us from harvest to harvest. Buy your garlic "seed" from a local or reputable seed source.

■ *Recommended Varieties*

Softneck garlic is the easiest to grow in our region and has the best storage life. 'Susanville' has generous-sized cloves on tight heads that store six to nine months. 'Early Red Italian' and 'Western Rose' are both long storage types, storing up to a year.

■ *When and Where to Plant*

Temperature: Garlic grows best in cool weather, at temperatures of 50°F to 60°F. Plant garlic bulbs outside in fall, applying a 4-inch layer of straw mulch. Bulbs will grow throughout the winter and will be ready to harvest in spring.

Soil: Garlic grows well in our soil. Add compost to the soil prior to planting. Garlic needs a well draining soil, or you can grow it in raised beds. The extra drainage prevents the bulbs from rotting.

Sun: Full sun.

■ *How to Plant*

Starting seeds indoors: Not recommended.

Planting outside: Plant garlic cloves 1 inch deep and 3 inches apart.

■ *How to Grow*

Water: Keep the soil moist during the first four weeks after planting—this is when the garlic cloves are growing roots. After that, they do not need extra water until spring. Resume watering once you see leaves start to appear. At the end of the life cycle, decrease watering to allow the bulbs to dry out.

Fertilizer: If you added compost to the soil before planting, you do not need to fertilize while the plants are growing. If you didn't add compost, topdress the area where garlic is planted with an organic fertilizer in the spring.

Pest control: Garlic plants are fairly pest tolerant. In fact, garlic cloves are used in many organic pest control products!

■ *When and How to Harvest*

Garlic is ready to harvest when the tops start dying back. When you see the leaves start to turn yellow, stop watering the bulbs and pull away the straw mulch to start toughening up the bulbs. Once the tops have died back, use a digging fork or trowel to gently dig up the bulbs. Cure the garlic by laying it out on a bench in a dry sunny spot, soil and tops intact, until they are thoroughly dry. Rub off the soil with gloved hands and store in a dark, cool location. You may braid the stems at this point to hang or pull them off to store just the heads. Although they look pretty, don't hang garlic in the kitchen. The light and moisture will cause rotting and desiccation.

GROWING TIPS

Invest in garlic "seed" sold locally or from a reputable seed source. When you harvest your crop, hold back small heads for seed for the next season.

Keep the garlic patch weeded—garlic bulbs don't compete well with weeds.

LEEK *(Allium ampeloprasum,* Porrum Group*)*

I had never cooked with leeks until I grew them in the garden. The seed catalog said they had a milder onion taste, which sounded perfect to me after experiencing the extra hot onions grown in our high desert summers—real eye waterers as I cut into them. Now leeks are a mainstay in the kitchen steamed, chopped, sautéed, roasted, grilled, and puréed. They are always welcome in the garden because we love them, and apparently, they love our garden too. Since planting out the tiny seedlings I had grown in the greenhouse our first gardening season, some leeks overwinter, popping up first thing in spring, and others self-sow every year. All that is left for us to do is to eat them!

■ *Recommended Varieties*

Plant 'Giant Musselburg' that doesn't mind the heat and is winter hardy. 'Roxton' is ready in 85 days. 'Lancelot' is virus tolerant and heat resistant.

■ *When and Where to Plant*

Temperature: Leeks take a long time to mature and they require cool temperatures to grow. They fare well when planted as transplants in early spring and allowed to grow during the summer and harvested in the fall. They can be left in the garden to harvest throughout the winter in milder climate areas and harvested in the late fall (October–December) in other regions.

Soil: Add compost to the soil before planting. Leeks grow best in loose soils full of organic matter. They do not mind alkaline soils.

Sun: Full sun.

GROWING TIPS

To get long, white stems, you have to hill leeks. As the plants grow, pile the soil up around the bottom leaves—just to the bottom of the leaf fork. This will encourage the plant to keep growing upward and forming new leaves at the top of the plant.

An alternative method in well-drained soils is to plant leeks in a shallow trench (4 to 6 inches deep). As the leeks grow, fill in the trench.

Keep the leek patch weeded and cultivate by hand to avoid damaging the roots.

■ *How to Plant*

Starting seeds indoors: Start seeds indoors (55°–75°F soil temp) eight to ten weeks before planting leeks outdoors. You can sow up to twenty seeds per 6-inch pot. When seedlings reach 4 inches tall, give them a crew cut to keep them at 3 inches. Repeat clipping (add the clippings to salad) every week or so to encourage root develop. Tease apart the roots when you're ready to plant outside.

Planting outside: Plant in the garden three weeks before last frost and space seedlings 6 inches apart, buried deeply. Harden off before planting in the garden.

Both the white root and the green leaves of the leeks can be eaten.

■ *How to Grow*

Water: For the best flavor, keep leeks evenly moist throughout the growing season. Do not let them dry out.

Fertilizer: Leeks are not heavy feeders. Sidedress with a balanced fertilizer every two months during the growing season but not during the dead of winter.

Pest control: Leeks are fairly pest free.

■ *When and How to Harvest*

Leeks mature in 85 to 120 days, depending on the variety. Once the stalks reach ½ inch in diameter, you can start harvesting them. If you've planted a lot of leeks (a 4-square-foot patch, for example), you'll have plenty of plants to harvest over a period of time. You can pull the younger plants to use in salads, omelets, and other quick-cook meals and save some plants to grow larger for use in soups and stocks. Harvest leeks by pulling up the entire plant. Most people cook with the tender, mild white part of the leeks. You can use the green tops for flavoring broth and soups, too.

LETTUCE *(Lactuca sativa)*

For a couple of years, I was known as the 'Lettuce Lady' while I was a participating farmer in our local farmer's market. It happened quite by accident. I was so swayed by all the pretty, varied types of lettuces in the seed catalogs and by the ease of growing the crop, that I got carried away. I planted the entire length of the garden in a 3-foot-wide swath with curly, deeply cut, green and tinted red romaines and buttery lettuces, interplanted with edible nasturtium, cilantro, basil, and bachelor's button. Now that I only grow for the two of us, I have tempered my lettuce planting into what I can fit into a small raised bed just outside the kitchen door.

■ *Recommended Varieties*

Look for heat-tolerant, slow to bolt types. I have best luck with leaf types, but 'Tom Thumb' is a small butterhead with a mild delicious buttery taste that is heat tolerant. Leaf types are easy to grow and you don't have to harvest the whole plant at once. Try 'Fleshy Trout', a romaine type green leaf with red spots. 'Ruby Red' has deeply cut leaves in bronze and 'Simpson' has curly green leaves, is slow to bolt and has a long refrigerator storage life.

■ *When and Where to Plant*

Temperature: Lettuce is a short-day, cool-season crop. In colder climates, sow seed indoors six weeks before the last frost, harden off seedlings, then plant in the garden two weeks before last frost. Repeat seed sowings every two weeks until the heat of the summer kicks in or throughout the entire season in cooler summer areas. For a fall planting, sow seeds outside six weeks before the first frost.

Soil: Lettuce grows fine in our soils. Because it is a heavy feeder, amend the bed with compost before planting.

Sun: Full to partial sun; sometimes lettuces will last longer into the summer if planted in partial shade.

Use scissors to snip off lettuce leaves, and it will grow back.

■ *How to Plant*

Starting seeds indoors: Sow seed thinly in rows in flats six to eight weeks before last frost. Use a cool soil, 45°F to 75° F. Thin seedlings to 3 inches apart and harden off before planting out.

GROWING TIPS

Cover lettuce seeds planted outside with seed-starting mix rather than garden soil. It is hard for tender lettuce seedlings to break through a hard soil crust.

Lettuce is great for container gardens. Interplant lettuce with tomatoes, peppers, basil, and edible flowers or plant many different types in one container for a salad bowl. It can be greenhouse grown for winter picking.

Planting outside: Sow seeds outdoors and cover with seed-starting mix. Press the soil down and water. (Pressing the soil cover down helps keep the seeds from floating away.) Sow head lettuce seeds with 1 inch between seeds. Thin to 4 inches after the plants have three sets of leaves. Thin to 12-inch spacing as the plants start to mature. Eat what you thin! Sow cut-and-come-again lettuces and leaf lettuces thickly—three seeds per inch. Grow lettuce under frost/snow protection into winter in milder winter climates.

How to Grow

Water: Keep the soil evenly moist.

Fertilizer: Lettuce likes to eat. As with all leaf crops, lettuce responds well to applications of composted chicken manure.

Pest control: Slugs are a major problem with lettuce. Spread diatomaceous earth around lettuce plants to create a barrier for slugs. Birds and mice will steal the seeds. If you have them flying or scurrying about, cover the seedbed with netting, anchored to the ground. After germination, remove the netting.

When and How to Harvest

Harvest head lettuce by pulling up the entire plant. Harvest leaf lettuce by using scissors to snip off leaves about ½ to 1 inch above the soil line. Cut intermittently throughout the rows. This encourages more growth between each swath before you cut again. Always harvest in the morning when the leaves are dry and the water content of the leaves is highest. Fill the bowl of a salad spinner or the sink with cold water and swish the leaves around. Dump them out into the strainer to drain. Spin, empty the bowl, then toss the lettuce about in the spin basket, spin again. Repeat. Lay the lettuce out on paper or linen towels for a half hour so, gently blotting the leaves to get as much moisture out as possible. Bag the lettuce or store in the spinner bowl in the refrigerator. If the leaves are properly dried, the lettuce will remain crunchy and crisp for up to two weeks.

PARSNIP *(Pastinaca sativa)*

I had never eaten a parsnip until a friend prepared and presented them to me mashed like potatoes, with a big dollop of melted butter in the center. It was love at first bite. Parsnips are relatives of carrots and have similar growing requirements. Parsnips, not eaten raw, are at their best roasted, steamed, sautéed, and mashed. They're high in vitamin C, fiber, and folate. They take awhile to germinate, but prefer to be left alone the remainder of their growing season.

■ Recommended Varieties

'Harris Model' is a reliable heirloom. 'Javelin' is resistant to canker and 'Gladiator' is a bit faster to germinate.

■ When and Where to Plant

Temperature: Plant parsnips outside as soon as the ground can be worked so they can mature into the fall.

Soil: Parsnips will grow fine in our alkaline soils but like a deep, workable, loose soil. Hard clay soils can cause forked roots. Dig compost deeply into the planting bed before planting.

Sun: Plant in full sun to partial shade.

Like carrots, parsnips need deep, loose soil to grow well.

GROWING TIPS

Buy seeds packed for your growing year. Parsnip seeds have a short shelf life.

Parsnips can take a while to germinate and don't like having to break through a soil crust. Plant radish seeds at the front and back of the rows and intermittently throughout. They will germinate quickly, mark the rows, and assist in breaking the soil crust to make way for the parsnips.

Parsnip leaves can cause a skin rash in some people. Always wear long sleeves and gloves when handling the plants.

How to Plant

Starting seeds indoors: Not recommended.

Planting outside: Soak seeds for 24 hours before planting. Sow seeds thickly outside—at a rate of three or four seeds per inch. Cover with seed-starting mix, and water. You might want to cover with frost cloth to help keep the soil from drying out during germination. Parsnips take up to 20 days to germinate, and the soil can't completely dry out during that time. Carefully thin seedlings to 4 inches apart once they germinate and have two sets of leaves.

How to Grow

Water: Keep the soil evenly moist, and water deeply so that the top 6 inches of soil are soaked when you water.

Fertilizer: Sidedress with a balanced fertilizer once a month during the growing season, or apply a slow-release fertilizer at planting time.

Pest control: Parsnips are fairly pest free. If rabbits and squirrels are a problem in your area, use a floating row cover for young plants.

When and How to Harvest

Parsnips are ready to harvest when the root tops are 1½ to 2 inches in diameter. Use a garden fork to loosen the soil around the parsnips to dig them up. It takes 120 to 150 days for parsnips to grow from seed to maturity, and by that time they're well rooted in. Parsnips always taste better when they've been exposed to cool weather.

Growing your own peas can save you money at the grocery store.

PEA *(Pisum sativum)*

"Eat your peas!" My parents delivered this edict as I tried to hide the offending things under a baked potato skin. My siblings and friends all shared my disdain for the veggie. I liked them straight from the garden and ate them like candy, but once they were boiled, they lost their enchantment (and all those vitamins). Now days, no pea nor pea shell (Edible pod peas are a delight!) that comes from our garden makes its way to the compost pile. We eat them raw still, right off the vine. They crunch with crispness, the juice flying out between our teeth, followed by the sugary sweet goodness from the shell and pea. Steamed, sautéed, stir fried, added to soups, stews, sauces, and casseroles—attributes from a plant that is a legume that fixes its own nitrogen. All we add is water.

■ Recommended Varieties

Sugar snap or snow peas have edible pods. Try 'Sugar Ann' that matures in 55 days. 'Oregon Sugar Pod II' is dwarf. 'Super Sugar Snap' is good for our short season areas and has mildew tolerance.

Try these varieties of shelling peas: 'Alaska' is very early. 'Lincoln' is for warm summer areas, less apt to set seed during the heat.

■ When and Where to Plant

Temperature: Plant pea seeds outside four to six weeks before the last frost. To shorten sprouting time and ensure that the peas don't succumb to fungal diseases, you can pre-sprout them for a week in a sprout bag or jar (or a plastic bag with moistened paper towels).

Soil: Peas do not need nutrient-rich soil, but they do need a water-retentive one. As legumes, they fix their own nitrogen—in effect making their own food.

Sun: Full sun.

■ How to Plant

Starting seeds indoors: Not recommended.

Planting outside: Use a hoe to dig rows 1 inch deep (even in raised beds). Plant rows 8 inches apart in raised beds and 18 inches apart in regular garden beds. Space seeds 2 inches apart when planting.

■ *How to Grow*

Water: Keep the soil evenly moist but not soaking wet. Do not allow the bed to completely dry out. In very dry soils, mulch the bed with straw once the seedlings are 6 inches tall.

Fertilizer: Do not overfertilize peas with nitrogen. Too much nitrogen can cause lots of green growth and no flowers. No flowers equals no peas! If you have poor soil, sidedress with a lower-nitrogen fertilizer when plants are 6 inches tall. The phosphorus and potassium will encourage good fruit development, and that's what you want to eat—the fruits!

Pest control: Aphids may occur. Use insecticidal soap according to package instructions to control the pests. Protect seeds from thieving birds and rodents. Cover with netting or wire until seedlings germinate and are up and thriving.

■ *When and How to Harvest*

Pick or clip off individual pea pods to harvest. Peas will be ready for harvest about 50 days after planting.

Harvest sugar snap peas when the pods are plump but still dark green in color. Harvest snow peas when the pods are still relatively flat. The flowers might still be hanging on to the ends of the pods of both types of peas when you harvest the pods.

Harvest shelling peas when the pods are plump but still dark green. Once the pods start to turn yellow, the sugars in the peas convert to starch, and they aren't tasty anymore.

GROWING TIPS

Place pea stakes or supports as soon as you see the plants germinating. They grow fast, and it's nearly impossible to wrestle a staking system into place once the plants are taller than 6 inches.

Dust the seeds with innoculant before planting according to package directions. Innoculants work well with all legumes, encouraging formation of nitrogen-fixing bacteria. The dusting also increases the harvest.

If you have poor germination rates, the peas could have succumbed to a fungal problem. Try again with a different variety that's disease resistant, or plant in a different area.

If you have tall plants but few peas, pinch off the growing tip of the plant to encourage more fruit production.

RADISH *(Raphanus sativus)*

When I think of the radishes of my youth, I think of the perfectly round, red, and sometimes peppery hot little orbs we were allowed to pull out of the garden just weeks after sowing the seed. Radishes were really the first of the veggies we could harvest from our backyard plot, a sign that there were more fruits to come from our early spring labors. They were at their best just as they formed the bulbs. The longer we left them in the garden, the tougher and hotter they became. Mom taught me how to make rose-like flowers out of the bulbs so they could still serve as a pretty garnish. We favor Daikon radishes that take longer to form their large, creamy white, 8- to 12-inch roots. The tops are used sautéed and the sweeter roots are eaten fresh, stir fried, sautéed, pickled, and steamed. But the red round radishes still make the best "flowers!"

■ *Recommended Varieties*

'Cherry Belle' is the typically round, red-on-the-outside, white-on-the-inside variety that matures in just 21 days. Milder 'French Breakfast' radishes have longer roots with red tops and white bottoms. Radishes also come in red, white, purple, and yellow hues. Daikon 'Minowase Summer'

Because radishes grow so quickly, they are a good plant for children to grow.

GROWING TIPS

Plant successive crops of radishes so that they don't mature all at once.

Plant radishes with cucumbers, melons, and squash. Allow the radishes to flower and they repel cucumber beetles. Radishes grow well in containers deep enough to support their mature root size.

doesn't mind the heat and produces white radishes 2 to 4 inches in diameter and 8 to 14 inches long.

When and Where to Plant

Temperature: Direct sow six weeks before the last frost and as soon as the soil temperature has reached 50°F. Sow successive crops every two weeks until daytime temps soar to over 90°F. For fall crops, sow seed as soon as daytime temps level out again (below 90°F), with successive crops sown from seven weeks before the first frost.

Soil: Radishes are not picky but as root crops, they need a well-drained soil.

Sun: Full sun.

How to Plant

Starting seeds indoors: Not recommended.

Planting outside: Sow successive plantings of radish seeds outside as soon as the soil can be worked. Plant seeds ½ inch deep and at the final spacing listed on the package. The seeds are large enough to space and thinning will not be required.

How to Grow

Water: Radishes aren't fussy, but they do need regular watering.

Fertilizer: Radishes are not heavy feeders. You should not have to fertilize.

Pest control: Use row covers to prevent flea beetles from attacking the plants. They eat on the roots, so if you harvest as soon as the radishes are ready, you shouldn't see any damage.

When and How to Harvest

Don't let the radishes linger. They taste best when harvested after three to four weeks of growth, when they are still relatively small. Daikon radishes can stay in the ground much longer, ready to harvest in 50 days.

SPINACH *(Spinacea oleracea)*

We love spinach so much that we use it alone as the star in a green salad and in place of lettuce on our sandwiches. It likes a cool growing season, turning bitter and bolting in the summer heat. As soon as the temperature starts to warm up and the days lengthen, the spinach season is over until fall. Successive plantings are key to a longer harvest period, along with regular watering, straw mulch to keep soil temps down and providing late afternoon shade in hot summer regions. Inevitably, all good spinach comes to an end, at which time, the New Zealand spinach sprouts from the previous season seed and take over the table until fall when it's time to sow spinach seed again!

■ *Recommended Varieties*

Look for slow to bolt types. 'Galilee' is an heirloom that is ready to harvest in just 35 days. 'Regatta' is resistant to mildew. 'Olympia' is good for spring or fall sowing.

■ *When and Where to Plant*

Temperature: Spinach will germinate in soil temperatures of 45°F to 75°F, so direct sow seed six weeks before the first frost, with successive plantings throughout cool summer regions. It grows best with air temperatures of

---

GROWING TIPS

Sow successive plantings to ensure fresh harvests of tender young leaves over a longer period of time.

Use drip irrigation or soaker hoses to provide steady water at the root zone and away from the leaves. Fungal diseases that plague spinach can spread through water on the leaves.

Once spinach sends up a flower stalk, pull up the plant, and compost it. Try New Zealand Spinach (*Tetragonia tetragonioides*), not a true *spinaceia* member, but treated as spinach just the same. It does not mind summer heat or sun, is even a bit drought tolerant, and produces a thicker, crunchier leaf on a trailing stem. Use the small leaves as salad greens, the larger ones are perfect for steaming, sautéing and stir frying. It will reseed itself for subsequent seasons. A great choice for an annual edible landscape groundcover.

Spinach is partially hardy but can be affected by frosts. If temperatures are forecast to be below 28°F, cover with frost cloth.

60°F to 65°F. In hot summer regions, sow seed as soon as soil warms and is workable. Successive sow until days warm beyond 80°F. Sow seed for fall crops six to eight weeks before the projected first frost.

Soil: Spinach grows fine in our alkaline soils, but it does enjoy organic matter. Incorporate compost into the soil before planting to ensure healthy growth.

Sun: Full sun.

How to Plant

Starting seeds indoors: It is best to direct sow spinach, but if you have a short spring season, you can start seeds indoors four weeks before planting outdoors.

Planting outside: Soak seeds overnight before planting outside. Sow fall crops directly outside into the garden. Space seeds 2 inches apart and thin to 6 inches apart after plants have three sets of leaves. Harden off transplants and plant 6 inches apart.

With a little planning, you can overwinter spinach in warmer regions.

How to Grow

Water: Spinach is not a heavy drinker, but keep the soil evenly moist and avoid wet/dry/wet/dry situations.

Fertilizer: Spinach is a leaf crop and a heavy feeder. Sidedress with a balanced fertilizer every two weeks during the growing season if you see leaves turning yellow.

Pest control: Prevent fungal problems by keeping water off the leaves. Use floating row covers to prevent damage from leaf miners.

When and How to Harvest

You can start harvesting spinach leaves three weeks after planting or when the plants have at least ten leaves on them. Cut the outermost leaves first, always leaving six leaves on the plant to produce sugars to help the plant keep growing. Use scissors or pinch off the leaves at the base of the leaf stalk. Spinach matures in about 40 days. You can also wait until that point and harvest the entire plant.

SWISS CHARD *(Beta vulgaris cicla)*

It's quite an amazing feat when a vegetable that is at home in the flower garden as it is sharing space in the vegetable plot, is delicious eaten raw or cooked, provides almost half of the daily requirement of Vitamin A and a quarter of the recommended Vitamin C, and only carries 7 (yes, I said 7!) calories per serving. Swiss chard is easily grown in all of the Rocky Mountain region, not minding the heat of summer or even a bit of frost. It grows in clumps, with large succulent puckered leaves on thick, white, red, orange, or yellow stalks that can be eaten fresh in salads when they are young. We like the large mature leaves with the stalks chopped up and sautéed with lots of garlic in olive oil.

■ *Recommended Varieties*

'Bright Lights', 'Rainbow', and heirloom 'Five Color Silverbeet' are multicolored mixes with stems in yellow, white, red, orange, pink, and green. 'Fordhook Giant' produces large green leaves with white stems.

Swiss chard is pretty enough to grow in a flower garden.

When and Where to Plant

Temperature: Swiss chard grows best in cool temperatures. Plant outside when soil temps have warmed to 50°F, and four weeks before the last frost with successive sowing every few weeks until six weeks before the first frost.

Soil: Swiss chard is not a picky plant and will grow in almost any soil. Add compost before planting.

Sun: Full sun to partial shade.

How to Plant

Starting seeds indoors: Not necessary.

Planting outside: Swiss chard grows to be fairly large. To sow seeds directly out into the garden, soak seeds overnight before planting. Plant one seed every 2 inches, ½ inch deep.

How to Grow

Water: Keep chard evenly moist.

Fertilizer: Fertilize with a balanced fertilizer every two to four weeks during the growing season.

Pest control: Use insecticidal soap to take care of any aphids or leaf miners that might attack.

When and How to Harvest

You can start harvesting Swiss chard leaves as soon as the plant has at least four or five leaves. Take the outermost leaves first, and allow the inner leaves to grow and provide sugars for the pant. Use a sharp knife, scissors, or hand pruners to cut the leaf stalks at the soil level. Dry the leaves as much as possible before storing to give a longer refrigerator shelf life.

GROWING TIPS

Thin plants once they are 3 or 4 inches tall so that there's one plant every 6 inches.

Leave Swiss chard in the garden throughout the summer, taking care to give it extra water. It can take a bit of frost and will overwinter with protection in USDA Zones 5 and above. Swiss chard makes a lovely container plant and an edible landscape border plant. Scatter seed in drifts or masses for a natural effect.

TURNIP *(Brassica rapa* spp. *rapa)*

Turnips are an extremely versatile, adaptable, easy-to-grow root crop in all Rocky Mountain regions. The tops, the greens, are ready to harvest just 30 days after direct sowing in the garden, making them a productive crop in areas with short growing seasons. They can handle the frost, giving them additional time to form their sweet bulbs, ready to dig just a month after harvesting the greens. Always stashed away in crates in my grandma's root cellar, they have a long storage life. Their creamy texture brings mashed potatoes to new heights and their sweetness enhances hearty winter stews.

■ *Recommended Varieties*

Heirloom large turnip varieties include 'Purple Top White Globe', and 'White Egg'. The 'All Tops' variety is grown specifically for turnip greens. 'Hakurei' is a small, white salad turnip that tastes good when shredded raw into salads.

■ *When and Where to Plant*

Temperature: Turnips will sprout when the weather is warm, but they need cool temperatures to mature if you want to harvest larger roots, rather than the tops. They do not like prolonged summer temperatures to

Turnips are grown both for their leafy green tops and their bulbous roots.

GROWING TIPS

Harvest every other plant when the roots are 1 inch in diameter. This will give you fresh turnips to eat immediately while allowing room for half of the harvest to grow larger roots. Harvest when bulbs are small, 3 to 4 inches for the sweetest roots.

Turnips may be container-grown in pots deep enough to accommodate their mature root size. They make good companions with onions, dill, chamomile, sage, and rosemary. Their foliage makes them a good choice for the edible landscape.

exceed 80°F. Sow seeds directly into the garden in cooler summer areas as soon as soil temps reach 55°F to 75°F, six weeks before the last frost. Sow for a fall crop in hotter summer regions when daytime temps have dropped below 80°F, six weeks before the first frost.

Soil: The biggest concern with turnips is to avoid planting them in exactly the same place that you grew cabbage and cabbage-family plants.

Sun: Full sun.

How to Plant

Starting seeds indoors: Not recommended.

Planting outside: Sow turnip seeds thinly (two seeds per inch) outside and cover with seed-starting mix. Turnips germinate quickly and will sprout within a few days. They also have a very high germination rate. If you plant a lot of seeds in a small area, expect to spend time thinning. Thin to 5 inches apart when plants are big enough to grab a hold of.

How to Grow

Water: Keep the soil evenly moist.

Fertilizer: Add compost to the bed before planting and you won't have to add additional fertilizer.

Pest control: Aphids can be controlled with insecticidal soap. Control flea beetles by using row covers.

When and How to Harvest

How you harvest depends on which part of the plant you want to harvest. Young, tender greens can be picked for salads when they are 2 to 4 inches tall. Pull up the young, tender roots when they are 2 inches in diameter and use them raw in salads. When the larger roots grow to 3 or 4 inches in diameter, they're ready to be pulled up and used for roasting and mashing. The greens can be braised or added to soups. Turnips have a sweeter flavor when allowed to mature when the weather is cooler.

Cool-season herbs cut for use as garnishes.

Cool-Season Herbs

Many of our favorite herbs grow best when the weather is cool. Dill, parsley, and cilantro are just a few of the everyday herbs that thrive during the early spring. Some of these herbs will hang on and grow through summer if provided with protection from the sun while others just physiologically won't stay vegetative once the days get longer—their fragrant leaves give way to flowers and seeds. In some cases, like dill and cilantro, the seeds carry more oils than the leaves and make wonderful dill seed and coriander for later use. Don't miss out on your favorite seasonings. Plant the herbs covered in this section during the cool-weather growing season.

Parsley

CILANTRO/CORIANDER
(Coriandrum sativum)

We grow drifts of cilantro up and down the length of the garden in a partially shaded location. Even in the heat of summer, I can cut the flowering stems, strip off the lower leaves, and chop up the tiny lacy white blooms to use in salads, salsa, soups, and other Mexican culinary delights. I allow the blooms to set seed, which gives it a whole new purpose. As the seeds and stems turn brown, I bend the plants over to lie on the ground, dispersing their seed to overwinter and to self-sow the following spring. Every foot or so, I pull the seed laden plants, roots and all, to harvest the seed to use whole. Some is also ground in the coffee grinder, when it becomes

We use the leaves of cilantro in salsas, but they are also tasty in salads and curries.

the most aromatic ground coriander you can imagine, not anything like what you find bottled in the supermarket. Sow it once and you will probably never have to sow it (or buy it!) again.

When and Where to Plant

Temperature: Cilantro grows best in temperatures of 50°F to 85°F. Sow seeds outside four weeks before the last frost. Allow the plants to set seed and it will self sow in early spring the following year.

Soil: The herb grows well in our slightly alkaline soils.

Sun: Full sun to partial shade. Planting in partial shade will extend the harvest window slightly.

How to Plant

Starting seeds indoors: Not recommended.

Planting outside: Plant seeds ¼ inch deep, with two seeds per inch.

How to Grow

Water: Keep seeds moist while sprouting, and avoid wet/dry/wet/dry periods while growing.

Fertilizer: Fertilize with a balanced fertilizer two weeks after germination.

Pest control: Cilantro has few pest problems but is susceptible to some fungal diseases spread through splashing water. Try to water the plants at the root zone and avoid splashing the water.

When and How to Harvest

To harvest leaves, snip the top off the plant. Store dry in the refrigerator and dry the excess leaves in a paper bag, then store in jars for use during the winter. Save coriander seeds by pulling up the whole plant once seeds have turned brown. Hang it upside down to dry over newspaper to collect the seeds.

GROWING TIP

The seeds are slow to germinate, so manage the weeds so they don't get out of control and out compete them for water and sun. Interplant cilantro in lettuce beds and with other vegetables. Rabbits, squirrels, and other critters don't care for them, and cilantro is an aphid deterrent too. Use cilantro in container gardens and in the edible landscape. The flowers are a bee and pollinator magnet.

Dill leaves can be used in salads and the seeds in flavoring.

DILL *(Anethum graveolens)*

I use dill seed for making lemon cucumber chips and in any dish containing cabbage. I use the feathery fine leaves to give some zip to green leafy salads. Coincidentally, dill is happy to share garden space with all of those veggies and is reported to improve their health and vigor. The companions make for one-stop harvesting. Dill seed carries the most flavor and stores well, maintaining their flavor, as do the leaves, when dried well before storing.

■ *When and Where to Plant*

Temperature: Seeds will germinate with soil temperatures of 50°F to 70°F. While the plant likes to grow during cool weather, it is frost sensitive. Plant dill seeds immediately after danger of frost has passed and do successive sowings throughout summer.

Soil: Like its relative the carrot, dill needs well-drained, loose soil.

Sun: Full sun.

■ *How to Plant*

Starting seeds indoors: Not recommended. Dill has a taproot, which makes it difficult to transplant.

Planting outside: Sow seeds thickly—two seeds per inch—and cover with seed-starting mix. The seeds can take up to two weeks to germinate. Keep the seeds moist while you look for growth.

How to Grow

Water: Keep dill evenly moist.

Fertilizer: No extra fertilizer is needed.

Pest control: Dill is susceptible to the same pests that eat carrots and parsnips, so don't interplant these crops. Keep an eye out for aphids and flea beetles.

When and How to Harvest

The leaves are most fragrant and delicious before the plants start to flower. Use kitchen scissors to snip off leaves. If you want to harvest seeds, allow the plant to flower. As the seeds are forming, keep a close eye on the plants. Pull up the plants and hang them upside down to dry over newspaper to collect the seeds.

GROWING TIPS

Dill needs protection from strong winds while it is small. It can get pretty tall and require support.

Don't be alarmed if you see caterpillars on the plants. They'll go away eventually.

For a steady supply of fresh, young leaves, sow several successive plantings of dill throughout early spring. It will re-seed itself in the garden. Be careful to pull out seedlings that might pop up in the carrot bed.

Try fernleaf dill, a dwarf type growing to 20 inches, in containers or in the edible landscape border.

A caterpillar munching on dill.

PARSLEY *(Petroselinum crispum)*

For many years, I thought of parsley as that green curly leaved garnish that I moved to the side of the plate to get to the "real" food. I don't know when I did the complete turn in my feelings about parsley. I know that now I am never without a clump of parsley in the garden and even container-grow them during the winter in the greenhouse so I always have some at the ready. I use flat-leaved parsley in the kitchen, fresh in salads of all types and steamed in sauces, soups, stews, and casseroles. Curly leaved parsley is front and center in the edible landscape, its ruffly, deep green, lush foliage making the perfect foreground border plant.

◼ *When and Where to Plant*

Temperature: Parsley grows best in cool early spring or late fall air temperatures of 60°F. You can plant parsley transplants outside as soon as the soil temperature warms to 50°F in early spring.

Curly parsley

Flat-leaf Italian parsley

Soil: Parsley grows best in our slightly alkaline soils that are well draining and high in organic matter.

Sun: Full sun to partial shade, especially in the hottest regions.

How to Plant

Starting seeds indoors: Seeds are difficult to germinate. Use transplants.

Planting outside: Plant 4 inches apart.

How to Grow

Water: Parsley needs regular watering.

Fertilizer: Parsley is a heavy feeder. Sidedress with a balanced fertilizer every four weeks during the growing season.

Pest control: Some butterfly caterpillars munch on parsley. Don't worry about them—they will eventually disappear.

When and How to Harvest

Keep parsley growing by frequently cutting the outermost leaves for kitchen use. While the plant is producing more leaves than you can eat, lay out the clean and dried leaves on paper towels or the drying racks until crispy. Store in glass jars, crumbling them as little as possible. The leaves retain the oils longer if whole and on the stem until use. Prolong leaf growth by cutting back the flower stalks for a time. Eventually parsley will flower, set seed, and die.

GROWING TIPS

Buy transplants locally. It can be interplanted in the garden with onions to help deter onion flies. It makes a lovely edible landscape plant and planted in the rose garden, it will repel rose beetles while making a great border plant. It works fine in containers of all sizes and types.

Marigolds serve to ward off pests and attract pollinators in this raised-bed garden filled with peppers. Mulch keeps moisture in the soil and helps with weed control.

Warm-Season Gardening Tips & Tricks

The warm-season vegetable gardening season in the Rocky Mountain region runs from May to September in the warmer valley and low desert areas. It runs from June to September in higher elevations.

Most of the warm-season vegetables and herbs that we grow are originally from tropical regions. They are tender to frost and don't grow well during cool weather. While they might hang on if air temperatures are above freezing, but if the soil is not yet warm, they won't germinate or grow.

Avoid planting warm-season crops too early. We usually get warm, spring-like days in April, and that is when we see plant starts in the nursery. However, we always get a late frost at the end of April and there is frost danger until Mother's Day, so don't be lulled into early spring fever. You can certainly buy, but keep the plants safe and harden them off, and don't plant until after the last frost and soil temperatures stabilize at 60°F to 65°F and nighttime air temperatures remain warm.

Watering During the Warm Season

Everything during the warm season is expedited, including water use. You might be able to get away with watering your cool-season vegetable garden every other day, but you will need to water every day during the warm season. The heat causes plants to use more water as the soil and roots warm up and water evaporates from the soil more quickly.

Mulching plants cuts down on watering frequency, cools the soil, and minimizes water loss through evaporation and wind erosion. Many summer vegetables are sensitive to wet/dry/wet/dry conditions. Provide deep, slow, regular watering (drip irrigation) directed at the roots of the plant to maintain moisture levels that will avoid problems such as blossom-end rot and splitting.

Planting for Pollination

We eat the vegetative parts of cool-season vegetables, like the beautifully colored leaves of Swiss chard and the juicy, sweet bulbs of onions. Warm-season vegetables produce the fruits, like tomatoes, peppers, and squash. To get fruits, flowers have to be pollinated by winged creatures, bees, flies, wasps, birds, and butterflies. Corn is a wind-pollinated plant, so it needs to be planted in rows or in blocks for pollination between plants to occur.

You can increase pollination rates by planting flowers in the vegetable garden. All plants in the aster family attract pollinators. Lettuce and radishes, if you let a few stay in the garden and flower, attract pollinators. Many herbs, if allowed to flower, also attract beneficial insects and pollinators. Leave space in the warm-season vegetable garden for interplanting flowers and herbs. The space won't be wasted.

Some plants that attract pollinators, beneficial insects, and/or enhance their garden companions are:

Basil	Mountain mint	Tarragon
Bee balm	Nasturtium	Thyme
Cosmos	Purple coneflower	Zinnia
Lettuce	Radish	
Marigold	Sunflower	

A row of pollinator plants near the vegetable gardens

Dealing with Pests

Many more pests are active during the warm season than during the cool season. It can be frustrating at times, dealing with so many pests. You'll see that many of the vegetable profiles have recommendations to "use floating row covers" to protect the plants. There are different remedies for pests, listed in individual plant profiles. However, the best ways to deal with pests have nothing to do with what to spray on the plants.

1. **Keep the plants healthy.** A healthy, nourished, thriving plant is better able to ignore a few aphids or pests and go on its way to producing fruits. Prepare the soil, incorporate compost to provide well-drained soils, give the plants their space needed to grow, and water them when they need it. Keep the garden clean of debris and weeds. Preventative and healthy horticulture practices will keep your plants thriving.

2. **Plant a variety of plants in the garden, plant groups of the same plant in many places throughout the garden, and interplant with companions.** Diversity is the key to luring beneficial insects and confusing harmful ones. A vegetable garden is not a natural ecosystem, but it can more closely mimic one if you introduce variety. The plant profiles list good garden companions and some serve as pest deterrents.

3. **Raise your threshold for pest damage.** A few munches out of the Swiss chard, a small worm hole in a pepper, a little blossom end rot, a cluster of squash bugs at the stem base of a pumpkin are not causes of concern in our kitchen. We just brush off the pest or cut out the offending blemish and eat the delicious fruits of our labor. I spend most of my efforts curtailing the attack of the birds and rodents who steal whole crops at one sitting and that bring their friends for any leftovers. The other pest that I do not abide is the tomato (and pepper, for they love those too) horned worm. They are disgusting creatures that have to be squished or fed to the neighbor's chickens or they will munch through an entire plant, leaves and fruit, overnight. You will decide how much damage and which critters you will tolerate and the ones you won't.

Planting a wide variety of vegetables, herbs, and flowers together confuses pests.

BEAN Bush and Pole Bean *(Phaseolus vulgaris)*

We eat a lot of beans at our house. Green beans, yellow wax bean, dried beans, and even soybeans have made their way from our garden to the table. Lush, climbing vines and short, strong bushes have been planted in the garden and in the landscape over the years. Their nitrogen-fixing ability benefits the soil, and their foliage and flowers beautify the arbor or trellis, providing shaded micro-climates for other crops to grow at their feet. Beans relish the warm, long, summer days. Green snap beans can be ready to harvest 50 days after planting. Dried beans stay on the vine until they are brown and dry and must be harvested before the first frost.

■ *Recommended Varieties*

Snap beans, bush type: 'Jumbo' is a cross that produces large 10-inch beans. 'Speedy' produces beans in 50 days. 'Golden Wax' is an heirloom that forms yellow stringless pods.

Snap beans, pole-type: 'Kentucky Blue', 'Kentucky Wonder' is an heirloom, 'Violet' is purple stringless, 'Heidi' is early, ready in 60 days.

Dried beans: 'Missouri Wonder' is an heirloom pole type, often grown climbing up corn. Beans are pinto-like. 'Snow Cap' is a half runner, shorter growing with beautiful beans half white and half brown with spots that hold their color after cooking. They have a mild flavor and silky texture.

GROWING TIPS

Don't jump the gun with beans. Wait until the soil has warmed to at least 60°F before planting.

Mulch beans with wheat straw, shredded newspaper, and other low-nitrogen materials to keep moisture levels even and weeds to a minimum.

Do not interplant beans with onions as they inhibit the bulb growth.

Interplant beans with corn to allow them to climb up the corn and to fix the nitrogen for the corn. Grow beans over your sunny trellis in your flower garden. Scarlet runner beans are beautiful ornamentals as well as edibles, and they can be eaten in the pod when young, eaten fresh and shelled when still tender, or eaten as dried beans.

Pole beans growing up a trellis

▪ *When and Where to Plant*

Temperature: The soil temperature at a 4-inch depth needs to be at least 60°F before planting beans. Keep your soil thermometer handy!

Soil: Add compost to the soil before planting. Beans grow fine in our soils.

Sun: Full sun; select an area for your pole beans on the north side of the garden so that they won't shade out the rest of your plants as they grow.

▪ *How to Plant*

Starting seeds indoors: Not recommended or needed.

Planting outside: Plant beans outside when the soil temperature is at least 60°F at a depth of 1 to 1½ inches. Space bush beans 12 inches apart, pole beans 6 inches apart. Provide supports for pole beans when they are 4-inches tall.

◼ *How to Grow*

Water: Beans are somewhat drought tolerant until they start flowering. Once plants start flowering, the beans should be kept evenly moist.

Fertilizer: Beans fix nitrogen, so they do not need high-nitrogen fertilizers. Once beans start flowering, fertilize once with a 0-5-5 or 0-10-10 fertilizer if phosphorous and potassium are needed.

Pest control: Pest problems include Mexican bean beetles, thrips, aphids, corn earworms, and stinkbugs. Row covers can keep beetles, stinkbugs, and corn earworms away from plants. Use insecticidal soap to control thrips and aphids. Interplant marigolds with beans to repel most pests. Protect seeds from marauding birds and rodents. When seedlings are 6 inches tall, the netting/wire can be removed.

◼ *When and How to Harvest*

Once pods start forming, it's time to harvest. Snap beans should be picked when the pods are still tender. Beans should be easy to snap off the plant and to break in half when they're ready to harvest. Pick in the morning when the plants have the highest moisture content. Beans taste best if eaten soon after harvesting, so pick them on the day you plan to eat them or blanch and freeze for up to one year. To keep plants producing, pick regularly. If beans are allowed to yellow on the plant, the plant will stop producing more pods.

To harvest pole types for shelling beans, wait until the pods start bulging and then pick before they turn yellow.

To harvest dry beans, allow the pods to dry on the plant. Pull off the pods or dig up the entire plant and hang it upside down to dry over a clean sheet. As the pods dry completely, the beans will pop easily and cleanly out of the pods. Store in a cool, dry place indefinitely.

Have fun in the garden by making artistic trellises for beans and other climbing vegetables.

CORN *(Zea mays)*

Corn is a wind-pollinated plant, so you have to grow the plants close together in blocks so the wind can blow the pollen from plant to plant.

For years, we attended the local fair to view the agriculture exhibits and horticulture displays. Adding to the excitement of the event: one particular food vendor that roasted ears of corn, still in their husks, on huge expansive wood-fired grills. Always our first stop, as the booth was strategically stationed just at the main entrance to the flower show, we were swooning as we bit into juicy, sweet corn on the cob, charred with grill marks and infused with hickory wood smoke. Needless to say, sweet corn was at the top of our garden list when we designed our garden plots. It has graduated in size to having its own designated garden, one it usually shares with "sister" (see below for "Three Sisters" growing) crops, beans and squash. Our first corn of the season always makes its way to the grill for that same "good as we got at the fair" taste.

■ *Recommended Varieties*

In cooler summer areas, grow corn varieties that grow in cool soil and that mature quickly. Suggested varieties include: 'Bodacious', 'Quickie', 'Precocious', and 'Earlivee'. Good varieties for gardeners with long hot summers include: 'Silver Queen', 'Sugar Dots', and 'Supersweet Jubilee'.

■ *When and Where to Plant*

Temperature: Sweet corn does not grow well in cold soil. Wait to plant until soil temperatures are 60°F, after the last frost.

Soil: If you grew peas in spring, plant corn in the same place (after you remove the peas). The corn will benefit from the nitrogen fixed by the peas. Or interplant with beans, also legumes. Before planting, add compost to the soil and work in a balanced slow-release organic fertilizer.

Sun: Full sun.

■ *How to Plant*

Starting seeds indoors: Not recommended or needed.

Planting outside: Wait until the soil has warmed up to plant corn. You will need to plant in at least three rows for pollination or in blocks or clusters of twelve or more plants. Sow seeds 6 inches apart in rows that are 18 inches apart.

■ *How to Grow*

Water: Corn requires consistent moisture through the growing season, more moisture when it starts to flower. If it is drought stressed, the leaves will roll up and the plants will take on a "pointy" appearance.

Fertilizer: Corn is a hungry plant. Prepare the planting area by adding compost and a slow-release fertilizer before planting. Fertilize with alfalfa meal and soybean meal when the corn is 2 feet tall and again when it starts to flower.

Pest control: There are many pests that attack corn plants. If you've had problems with earworm, treat ears with a combination of *B.t.* and mineral oil (1:20) five days after silks emerge. Place five drops on the silks at the end of each ear.

■ *When and How to Harvest*

Sweet corn is ready to harvest when the juice that squirts from a kernel pierced by a fingernail is milky white and after the silks (hairs on the ears) are completely brown. You can hold the corn stalk in one hand and grasp the ear in the other hand, jerking the ear off the plant without yanking the plant out of the ground.

GROWING TIPS

Intercrop with beans and squash for "Three Sisters" planting. When corn is 4 inches tall, sow a bean seed at the base, with squash seeds planted in between the rows. The beans will fix nitrogen in the soil and use the corn for support. The squash will sprawl along the ground, providing a living, soil-cooling mulch on the soil.

Cut off any small plants that sprout from the base of the main stalk. These suckers will sap nutrients from the main plant.

Harvest promptly when the corn is ripe. Overripe corn is tough and chewy. It may be frozen in the husk for up to 6 months. Or remove the husks and silks, blanch, and freeze whole cobs or kernels in airtight bags to store up to one year.

CUCUMBER *(Cucumis sativus)*

There is a cucumber for every cucumber lovers' taste and purpose. Over seasons of growing our own, we have discovered what our perfect cucumber is, so that is the only one we grow. Lemon cucumbers, an heirloom dating back to 1894, are ready to harvest in 60 days from transplants. It is at the peak of crispy sweetness when harvested as it reaches the size of a large lemon. The cucumber is almost perfectly round with pale green flesh that turns golden lemon yellow when ripe. The seeds are large, but we the eat the peel and rind portions, scooping out and composting the seeds, then cutting the rind into strips or chunks. Lemon cukes remain crispy after pickling the rinds and have a mildly sweet flavor. There are many cucumber types available, disease resistant, good for slicing and for pickling. Cucumbers can take the heat and languish in the sun to grow in the kitchen garden, in the edible landscape as a groundcover, and in containers.

■ *Recommended Varieties*

Look for short season cucumbers if you garden in cooler summer regions. 'Bush Pickle' (ready in 45 days) is a dwarf, compact grower at 24 to 30 inches wide and tall. It's a good multipurpose cuke sliced fresh or pickled. 'Raider' is disease resistant (see below) and ready to harvest in 52 days. 'Lemon' cucumber is a semibush type, so it can be trellised or trailed. 'Patio Snacker' is a bush type and good in containers. 'Manny' grows in a heated greenhouse in cold winter areas, requiring lower light levels.

Cucumber varieties are bred for disease resistance. Consult with your local Cooperative Extension to see what resistance you need for your area. CMV means the cucumber variety is resistant to cucumber mosaic virus; DM means resistance to downy mildew, S is scab resistant; PM means resistant to powdery mildew, and ALS is resistant to angular leaf spot. DM resistance is very important for season-long cucumber production in areas with summer rains or high humidity.

Growing cucumbers up a trellis saves space in the garden.

■ *When and Where to Plant*

Temperature: Plant cucumbers when all danger of frost has passed and the soil is at least 60°F. Cucumbers benefit from being trained to grow up a trellis on a dark-colored wall and benefit from black plastic mulch, water bottles, and other heat-enhancing tricks if your soil is slow to warm in spring.

Soil: Cucumbers grow fine in our slightly alkaline soils but need a well draining soil. They are also heavy feeders and use a lot of water. Incorporate compost into the soil before planting in order to grow healthy plants.

Sun: Full sun.

■ *How to Plant*

Starting seeds indoors: Start indoors up to four weeks before planting outdoors. Plant in peat pots that you can plant directly outside into the soil with minimal root disruption.

Planting outside: Sow seeds or plant transplants outside when the soil temperature is at least 60°F and all danger of frost has passed. Allow 8 to 12 inches between plants.

■ *How to Grow*

Water: Cucumbers are heavy drinkers. Keep the soil evenly moist during the entire growing period. These plants need more water than almost any other vegetable. Place drip tubing or soaker hoses along the base of cucumber plants to help deliver a steady stream of water at the roots. Straw mulch cools the soil, holds in moisture, and gives a clean surface for vines and fruit. Cucumbers can be container and greenhouse grown.

Fertilizer: Cucumbers need a lot! Sidedress cucumbers every two weeks during the growing season with a balanced fertilizer.

Pest control: Cucumber beetles and pickleworms are the peskiest pests to attack cucumbers. Neem oil and pyrethrum are two organic pesticides that can help control the pests. Interplant with radishes that are allowed to go to seed to repel beetles.

■ *When and How to Harvest*

Once cucumber fruits start forming, keep your eyes peeled for fruits that need to be picked. Fruits left unpicked will also stimulate the plant to stop fruiting. Harvest cucumbers when they reach mature size and color as specified on the seed packet. Use pruners to cut the fruits off, leaving 1 inch of stem on the end of the fruit. (This minimizes water loss after harvest.)

EGGPLANT *(Solanum melongena)*

There are hundreds of eggplant varieties that cover the entire color wheel and come in as many differed sizes and shapes. It got its roots (ha!) in India, then spread to other warm regions, Spain, Greece, and the Mediterranean. Due to its origins, eggplant is a heat lover, needing 80°F air temps just to germinate. In desert regions, it thrives with direct sowing, but in other cool summer short season areas, you will need to start the seeds early, then plant out hardened-off transplants. You only need one to three plants to supply each diner with eggplant for a season. Experiment with other types that produce smaller fruits, pick when small and explore new ways to prepare this exotic looking fruit. There is even a recipe for eggplant cake!

■ Recommended Varieties

Choose eggplant varieties with short seed to harvest days. Heirloom 'Korean Red' has small sweet green fruits that mature to red, ready in just 54 days. 'Casper' is a long white type. 'Early Long Purple' is, you guessed it, deep purple. 'Rosa Bianca' is pinkish lavender with white fruit and 'Japanese White Egg' is creamy white and ready in 65 days.

■ When and Where to Plant

Temperature: Eggplants need soil and nighttime air temperatures to be at least 65°F to grow. You can plant outside a bit earlier but may need to provide some protection by tunnels or hoops covered with grow cloth or black ground cloth to increase heat levels around the plants.

Soil: Add compost to the soil before planting, and plant in well-drained locations.

Sun: Full sun.

■ How to Plant

Starting seeds indoors: For most Rocky Mountain areas, start seeds indoors six to ten weeks before planting outside. Provide a warm soil (70°F) by using a heat mat and bright natural light or grow lights for strong plants.

Planting outside: Plant transplants outside after all threat of frost has passed, with 12 to 18 inches between plants. (You can get away with closer spacing in raised beds—12-inch centers work in these.)

■ How to Grow

Water: Eggplants need a large, consistent supply of water. Use drip irrigation tubing or soaker hoses around plants for the best result.

Fertilizer: Feed eggplants every two weeks with a balanced fertilizer. They like to eat.

Pest control: Many pests and diseases call eggplants home. Colorado potato beetles, tomato hornworms, and flea beetles are the worst insect offenders. Look for the orange eggs of the Colorado potato beetle on the undersides of the leaves, and wash the leaves with water or crush the eggs to control them. Specific strains of *Bacillus thuringiensis* (*B.t.*) are effective on adult beetles. The beetles are repelled by beans, so these make good garden companions. Keep an eye out for tomato hornworms and handpick them off (gross, but effective).

Eggplants come in different shapes and sizes. Look at your seed packet to tell what they're supposed to look like when ripe so that you know when to harvest.

■ *When and How to Harvest*

Consult the seed package to determine the size and color to look for when harvesting. If you leave the fruits on the plant too long, they'll grow big seeds and become bitter tasting. Ripe eggplants have shiny skin. If the skin is dull, they're past their prime, and they should be cut up, then composted. Use a knife or pruners to pick the fruits, leaving at least ½ inch of stem.

GROWING TIPS

Eggplants (the fruits) are heavy. Stake plants individually (one stake per plant, placed next to the stem and tied) to support the plants and keep the fruits from sitting on the soil.

If you've had problems with insects, one way to thwart them is to plant groups of the same vegetable in different areas of the vegetable garden. The pests might find one group, but will leave the others alone.

Eggplants can be container and greenhouse grown.

ONION *(Allium cepa)*

For easiest growth and storage, grow onions from sets to get a jump start on the season.

I grow and use as many onions as I do garlic. I was raised just miles from the home of the famed 'Walla Walla' onion, a requirement for any dish prepared using venison, the main source of protein of my childhood. While I no longer have access to venison, onions are added to every sort of savory dish I concoct, and I play up their sugary sweetness by caramelizing onions for burgers and sandwiches. We grow some sort of onion in the garden every year, rotating their location from season to season. Bulb types need a longer growing season, from 60 to 120 days, but store well, and bunching onions are ready to harvest just weeks after planting. Upon planting the bulbettes (started in the greenhouse) in early spring, I apply drip irrigation tubing, a thick layer of straw mulch, and don't give them another thought until harvesting them at summer's end.

■ Recommended Varieties

Bunching types: 'White Sweet Spanish', 'Long White Summer Bunching' (will often survive mild winters), 'Deep Purple', 'Feast'
Bulb types that store well: 'Red Bull', 'Copra', 'Talon'
Shallots: 'Ambition', 'Conservor', 'Dutch Yellow', 'French'

■ When and Where to Plant

Temperature: Plant onion sets for bulbs or seeds for bunch types outside three weeks before the last frost. Plant onion seed in fall to overwinter in mild winter Zones 6 and above.
Soil: Onions grow best in well-drained soils. Dry soils produce more pungent onions.
Sun: Full sun.

■ How to Plant

Starting seeds indoors: Start onion seeds indoors eight weeks before you plan to transplant them outdoors. Sow up to 100 seeds in a 6-inch pot. When seedlings reach 4 inches, give them a crew cut to keep leaves to 3

GROWING TIPS

Make sure you are purchasing varieties with proven track records in your area. Contact your local Cooperative Extension for recommendations.

Bulb and bunching onions can be grown in containers. They make good garden companions with tomatoes, lettuce, and summer savory. In the edible landscape, plant them with roses to help thwart off pests.

inches tall. This encourages strong root development. Repeat as needed until hardening off.

Planting outside: If planting seeds, you can sow up to four weeks earlier than if you are planting transplants. Plant bunching onions close together (2 inches apart) and bulbing onions 6 inches apart. Apply a 2- to 3-inch layer of straw mulch.

How to Grow

Water: Onions don't require a lot of water, but they do need even moisture. Dry soil will cause the onion to produce two bulbs instead of one. Increase watering as the bulb begins to form and swell. Decrease watering in the last two weeks before harvesting.

Fertilizer: Incorporate a balanced, slow-release fertilizer into the planting bed before planting onions. Alternately, spread 3 inches of compost on the bed the previous autumn and rototill in before spring planting.

Pest control: Onion root maggots are the most problematic pests for onions. Good sanitation, removal of dead plant leaves, and crop rotation help control onion maggots.

When and How to Harvest

Harvest bunching onions when they are ⅓ inch in diameter. Pull up the entire plant and chop it up for use in salads, soups, stews, and sandwiches.

Prepare to harvest bulb onions when their leaves start to turn brown. When you see the browning, bend the leaves to one side to allow more sunlight to toughen up the bulbs. A week later, gently lift (don't dig them out yet!) the bulbs with a digging fork to break the roots from the soil and to continue to harden them off. Stop irrigating at this point. Dig the entire bulb up two weeks later, knock off large clumps of soil and lay them out in a sunny dry place to finish curing. Don't allow them to get wet during the curing process. Pull off any remaining foliage, leaving as much papery skin as possible. Store in a cool, frost free, dry location. They will store for six to eight months if properly cured.

Most of our Rocky Mountain region is a great place to grow peppers.

PEPPER *(Capsicum annuum)*

Peppers are always on our garden list of must-haves, and they are one of the most persnickety crops we grow. They are true heat lovers, refusing to put out new green growth until soil temps remain well above 65°F and nighttime temps don't drop any lower than that. They love the sun to keep their "feet" warm, but as they set fruit, the larger leaves may not provide enough shade to protect the peppers from sunscald. When I see a black hotspot on the fruit, I add a layer of light shade cloth until the temps cool down. When their needs are fulfilled, they grow thick stalks with branches up and down the stem. They are built to support themselves, unless wind gusts kick up, in which case I run out to the garden, stakes and twine in hand, to help them out a bit. The extra effort, for what I consider to be my high maintenance garden darlings, is worth every bit of it, when I harvest the shiny green, orange, yellow, and red spicy hot or sweet fruits.

■ *Recommended Varieties*

Some tried and true varieties: 'Felicity' (Jalapeno), 'Flamingo' (wax pepper), 'California Wonder' (bell pepper), 'Wonder Bell' (bell pepper), 'Hungarian Wax' (wax pepper/ banana pepper), 'Italian Pepperoncini' (sweet), 'Anaheim' (hot), 'Ancho' (hot), and 'Miniature' bells (small sweet).

■ *When and Where to Plant*

Temperature: Peppers need warm soil to grow—at least 65°F to 75°F at a depth of 4 inches. Do not plant outside until all danger of frost has passed.

Soil: Peppers grow fine in Rocky Mountain soils. Bell and sweet peppers are heavy feeders, so add compost to the soil before planting.

Sun: Full sun.

■ *When and How to Plant*

Starting seeds indoors: Start seeds indoors eight to ten weeks before you plan to transplant outside. You want the transplants to be at least 6 inches tall before planting outside. For strong transplants, use a heat mat under the flat that is set at 75°F. Provide bright sunlight or a grow light. When plants sprout and have their first leaves, leave the grow lights on the plants for at least sixteen hours per day. When the first true leaves (second set of leaves) appear, transplant seedlings into 4-inch pots. Fertilize once a week with ½-strength water-soluble balanced fertilizer. Harden off the plants by bringing them out of the greenhouse on sunny days but put back in the house until all danger of frost has passed, and then plant in the garden.

Planting outside: Plant peppers outside when soil temperatures are at least 65°F. Plant transplants 12 inches apart.

Some bell peppers can be left on the plant longer for a red or orange color.

■ *How to Grow*

Water: Bell and sweet peppers thrive with regular water. If they go through wet/dry/wet/dry cycles (irregular watering), they develop blossom-end rot, a condition in which the end of the fruit opposite the stem rots. Hot peppers are more drought tolerant, however, the drier the soil, the hotter the peppers!

Peppers, if interplanted with basil, are said to have sweeter fruit. Jalapeños are easily container grown as their smaller compact size needs no staking. Also good in the edible landscape used as a border plant. Sweet bells can be grown in 5-gallon or larger pots with support.

Fertilizer: Feed peppers with a balanced fertilizer when they start blooming and again four weeks later.

Pest control: Peppers are relatively pest free, especially hot peppers.

Banana peppers are easy to grow!

GROWING TIPS

Use drip irrigation tubing or soaker hoses around pepper plants to provide consistent and deep watering. Bell and sweet peppers thrive when mulched with shredded newspaper, straw, and other organic mulches. Stake plants or cage individually when they grow to heights of 18 inches or taller. Wear gloves when harvesting hot peppers.

■ *When and How to Harvest*

Read the seed packet or label to see when your peppers will be ready to harvest. There will be an indication of days to maturity (after transplanting outside), as well as pictures that show you what the "finished product" looks like. Red, orange, purple, and yellow bell peppers are green when immature, turning colors as they ripen. Green bell peppers are ripe when they reach their harvest size, usually about 60 days after planting out. If fruit hasn't formed by the end of August, then there won't be enough time to form and ripen before first frost. The longer peppers grow, the sweeter or hotter they get.

POTATO *(Solanum tuberosum)*

The potatoes we buy in the grocery store and the potatoes we dig from our garden are, in taste and texture, two different creatures. The red potatoes are sweeter, the fingerlings more creamy, and even the plain, taken-for-granted russets take on a distinctive, earthy, rich flavor. Growing your own spuds starts with a reliable, preferably organic "seed" source. Buy from your local garden center or online from a reputable, organic certified supplier. They need some space in a well-draining soil with some organics added at planting time. Keep them "hilled" and apply water. Properly harvested, cured, and stored, they will keep for months.

■ Recommended Varieties

Purchase seed potatoes that are certified disease free or organic and you'll be in good shape. 'Yukon Gold', 'All Blue', and 'Mountain Rose' and 'Sangria' are good varieties. Fingerling potatoes such as 'Russian Banana' or 'French Fingerling' are also good choices.

■ When and Where to Plant

Temperature: Potatoes sprout when the soil temperature is between 50°F to 70°F. Plant outside as soon as the ground can be worked, about one week before last frost is fine.

Soil: Loose, well-drained soil.

Sun: Full sun.

■ How to Plant

Planting outside: Pre-sprout (chit) the seed potatoes before planting out. Set the potatoes, eye side up, in a flat in a well-lighted (not full sun) window in a warm (70°F) area for one to two weeks before planting. Roots will form from the eyes. Plant in trenches a foot deep and cover potatoes with 4 to 6 inches of soil. Leave 8 (fingerlings) to 12 inches between plants.

■ How to Grow

Water: Keep potatoes evenly moist but not soggy. Let the soil dry out between waterings.

Fertilizer: Apply low-nitrogen, high-phosphorous fertilizer at the time of planting. (Bone meal works well.)

Pest control: Diseases are the main problem. Start with disease-free seed potatoes. There are a variety of pests that attack potatoes. If you suspect a problem, contact your Cooperative Extension.

Digging for potatoes is a great way for children to get involved in the garden.

Hilling: Potatoes need to be "hilled," which is mounding the soil around the plant stem 2 inches up at a time. Mound when plants reach 6 inches tall and continue to mound every two weeks until plant leaves touch each other. The trench will be filled in and the hills will leave about 12 to 18 inches of growth above ground.

How to Harvest

Harvest early potatoes by carefully removing some of the soil from around the stem and feeling around for immature potatoes. The rest of the potatoes are ready to harvest when the tops of the plants start dying back in early autumn. Lay the freshly dug potatoes in the sun, with the dirt on them, for a few hours to toughen up the peel. Then, with a light touch, rub the dirt off the potato and store in a cool, dark, airy location. Burlap bags work well for storage.

GROWING TIPS

Don't let the soil around potatoes stay soggy.

Keep up with hilling—check plants every two to three weeks as they grow.

SUMMER SQUASH *(Cucurbita pepo)*

Mention "summer squash" and people hold up their hands in the "whoa!" position, visions of giant zucchini in their heads. To be sure, a little bit of zucchini goes a long way, with just one or two plants per zucchini-eating person being the recommended quantity to grow. There are many other types of summer, heat-loving squash to grow and to eat. We favor 'Lemon' squash, a beautiful yellow, round squash that doesn't get much bigger than a tennis ball and yellow crooknecks that have more "meat" than they do seed. They all have a mild taste, but some are sweeter than others and some are firmer in texture. They all are at their best picked just when the flowers drop off the small fruits. Steam, sauté, grill, grate for muffins, cookies, and cakes to use every last one!

■ *Recommended Varieties*

Look for varieties that are resistant to cucumber mosaic virus, powdery mildew, and downy mildew if those diseases are prevalent in your area. Many heirlooms have toughened up over many seasons. Summer squashes include all of the thin-skinned squashes that are suitable for eating cooked or raw. 'Delta' is resistant to powdery mildew. 'Sunburst' is a patty pan, a scalloped squash, yellow with a green cap that keeps its creamy texture from baby size, 2 to 3 inches to a mature 6- to 8-inch size. 'Lemon' squash is an

Harvest summer squash right after the flower on the end of the fruit wilts.

heirloom with built-in resistance to pests. 'Tigress' is virus tolerant and ready in just 49 days. Zucchini types are 'Costata Romanesco', 'Easy Pick Gold', and 'Eight Ball'. 'Patio Star' is a bush type and perfect for containers.

When and Where to Plant

Temperature: Squashes need warm soil to grow. Plant outside after all danger of frost is passed. Use black mulch around the plants to keep the temperature elevated around them if you are in a cool summer area.

Soil: Add compost to the soil before planting.

Sun: Full sun.

How to Plant

Starting seeds indoors: Squash plants are difficult to transplant. If you live in an area with a short growing season, start seeds indoors four weeks before planting outdoors. Plant the seeds in peat pots or biodegradable pots that you can plant directly in the ground with minimal disruption to the roots.

Planting outside: Sow seeds outside when soil temperatures are at least 65°F. Plant two to three seeds per hole, 1 inch deep. When seedlings are 3 inches tall, use scissors to thin to two plants per 12 inches. As plants grow, you can further reduce to one plant per 18 or 24 inches. (Overplanting slightly gives you more plants to work with if you have problems with pests.)

How to Grow

Water: Keep squashes evenly moist. It helps if you mulch the garden after the plants germinate.

Fertilizer: Sidedress with a balanced fertilizer every three weeks during the growing season.

Pest control: Squash bugs, squash vine borers, cucumber beetles, and squash beetles plague squash plants. Use row covers when plants are young to protect plants from the flying pests. Raise the covers for two hours in the early morning a few days a week to allow insects to reach the flowers for pollination. Interplant with nasturtiums or radishes that are allowed to set seed to deter pests and to attract pollinators.

When and How to Harvest

Once summer squash plants start producing, you need to check the plants daily for fruits to harvest. Summer squash tastes better when harvested young. The flowers are edible too. Summer squash can be dried, frozen, or canned. The texture will be sacrificed, but the mild flavor is maintained.

SWEET POTATO *(Ipomoea batatas)*

Sweet potato oven French fries elevate the French fry to a whole new level. They are a guilt-free way to eat fries with your burger, while making the healthy choice. No longer relegated to the traditional canned sweet potato casserole with marshmallows of our childhood, sweet potatoes, freshly dug from the garden, are in a food class all their own. The plant got its origin in South America, where long warm growing seasons created lush, heavily foliaged vines. Packed in Vitamin A, rich in beta-carotene, and full of fiber, sweet potatoes can be baked, boiled, steamed, sautéed, sliced, diced, and mashed. They store for a few months if kept in a cool (55°F) dark location and if they are blanched and frozen, they keep for a year. They are easy to grow if you have long hot summers and are even a bit drought tolerant, making them tough enough to withstand the elements in low and high desert regions.

Recommended Varieties

Look for these disease-resistant, short-season varieties of sweet potatoes.

Beauregard: Resistant to diseases, not nematodes, 95 days to high yields, good storage

Centennial: Resistant to root knot nematode and wireworm, 90 days, long-time proven performer

O'Henry: white fleshed, 90 days

Georgia Jet: good in colder regions, 90 days

'Bunch' Porto Ricos: bush type, good for containers and small spaces, 100 days

When and Where to Plant

Temperature: Plant slips outside when the soil temperature is at least 65°F and all danger of frost is passed. Consult the frost tables for your area (your local Cooperative Extension will have current information) before planting sweet potatoes. High Mountain elevation sweet potato growing might not have enough frost-free days to mature. Warm the soil up by applying a layer of black groundcover cloth or plastic two to three weeks before planting. They can take a bit of light frost at the end of their growing season. With protection, you can extend the growing season to get them to harvest size before winter weather arrives.

Soil: Sweet potatoes prefer a more acidic soil than we have, so incorporating peat moss to a depth of 12 inches will help the crop get off to a start. They like a sandy, fast-draining soil, so if you have poor drainage, plant slips in raised beds or in deep containers. Begin seasonal applications of organic matter into heavy soils to build the soil drainage capabilities.

Sun: Full sun.

■ *How to Plant*

Starting indoors: Grow them from slips or from sprouted roots from other sweet potatoes. You can also buy transplants.

Planting outside: Plant slips or transplants outside when the soil temperature remains at least 65°F. Sweet potatoes really need hot weather, or they'll just sit in the ground. The shorter the frost-free growing season, the more attention you will have to give to maintaining warm soil temperatures. Begin with well-established transplants. Plant slips 4 inches deep and 12 inches apart in rows 36 inches apart.

■ *How to Grow*

Water: Water while plants are establishing themselves (the first couple of weeks). After that, the plants will not need much extra water unless there is no rain for more than a week at a time.

Fertilizer: Sweet potatoes are not heavy feeders.

Pest control: Sweet potatoes are largely pest free, especially if you plant resistant varieties. If you grow sweet potatoes each year, you can keep problems at bay by rotating where you plant them each year. Deer love sweet potatoes and can be a major pest. In areas with high deer pressure, fencing may be necessary.

■ *When and How to Harvest*

Sweet potatoes are ready to harvest about 100 days after planting or when the roots are at least 3 inches in diameter. Cut and remove the vines to compost, and then gently dig around the plants and pull up the roots. Be very careful not to bruise the potatoes, as even slight bruising can lead to rot. Allow the roots to dry on top of the soil for a day. After curing for a day outside, pick up the roots and bring them inside. Cure the potatoes inside for a week before putting them in storage. Set the potatoes out in a warm, dark room (85°F to 90°F) with high humidity. This allows any cuts or bruises to heal. Then move them to a cool (55°F to 65°F), dark area and leave them alone until you're ready to use them.

Sweet potatoes grow best in the long growing season and warm weather.

TOMATILLO *(Physalis ixocarpa)*

Tomatillo hails from South America. That news alone should give clues as to their preferred growing conditions. In the Rocky Mountain region, they should be started from seed indoors at the same time you start your tomato and pepper seeds. I usually start mine in February so that I plant out strong, healthy, hardened-off, and ready to flower quart-sized pots after all danger of frost is passed. Tomatillos have similar cultivation needs of tomatoes, but tomatillos are ready to harvest sooner, maturing just 65 days after sowing seed. The fruit is encapsulated in a papery husk, which gives them a long refrigerator shelf life of up to six weeks. Tomatillos are tart and acidic in their juvenile state, making them a perfect match when pared with avocados in guacamole and salsas. Their smooth texture adds character to sauces. Tomatillos, when added to dishes that carry some heat from hot chili peppers, will "cool" the dish down.

■ *Recommended Varieties*

'Tomatillo Verde' is a smaller, sweeter variety of tomatillo. 'Mexican Strain' has savory fruit that is large and drops from the vine when it is ripe in about 65 days. 'Rio Grande' is an heirloom. It is a strong bushy type that does not need staking.

Wait until the husks turn brown and papery before harvesting tomatillos.

▧ *When and Where to Plant*

Temperature: Tomatillos like it hot. Plant transplants outside as soon as all danger of frost has passed.

Soil: Tomatillos aren't picky plants but will grow best in well-drained soil. If you have clay soil, amend with compost before planting.

Sun: Full sun.

▧ *How to Plant*

Starting seeds indoors: Start seeds inside six to eight weeks before you plan to plant outside. For strong seedlings, use a heat mat under the seedling flat and grow in bright natural light or use grow lights 2 inches above the plants (moved up as they grow).

Planting outside: Plant hardened-off transplants outside when all danger of frost is passed, leaving 12 inches between each plant. Tomatillos may require a cage or staking.

▧ *How to Grow*

Water: Keep tomatillos evenly moist.

Fertilizer: Sidedress with a balanced fertilizer four weeks after planting.

Pest control: Keep an eye out for pests that attack tomatoes, such as tomato hornworms, aphids, and cutworms. You can protect plants from cutworms by loosely wrapping the bottom 3 inches of the stems with newspaper.

▧ *When and How to Harvest*

Pick tomatillos off the plants when the husks start to dry out and turn light brown.

GROWING TIPS

Place tomato cages around individual plants to keep them from flopping over. For a bushier plant, pinch off the top of the plant to encourage side sprouts.

If growing tomatillos from seed, hill the soil up around the bottom 6 inches of the stem as the plant grows. If planting transplants, plant 4 or 5 inches deep to encourage rooting from the stem.

TOMATO *(Lycopersicon esculentum)*

When fellow gardeners ask, "How's the garden?" they immediately follow with, "How are your tomatoes?" Tomatoes are the stars of my garden. There is such a drastic difference in taste and texture between the tomatoes you buy and the ones you pluck from the vine. Even in my worst tomato year, when the skins are tough and the cores are hard, the sweet, acidic juicy flavor of my homegrown tomatoes beats anything I can find at the market. I grow heirlooms for their tried and true performance, high acidity that is good for canning, and so that I can collect the seed from favorites for subsequent season's planting. I like the hybrids and varieties, bred to ward off disease, produce high yields, and to have strong structures. I grow way more tomatoes than what I can preserve by canning, saucing, freezing, and drying, but my neighbors are always grateful when I show up on their doorstep with a basket full of red, yellow, green, orange, and multicolored fresh-from-the-vine tomatoes.

■ *Recommended Varieties*

In selecting tomato types to grow, consider days to maturity, space available, in what ways your family likes to eat tomatoes, and if certain diseases are prevalent in your area, what disease-resistance the variety carries. Consult your Cooperative Extension or other gardeners and farmers for recommendations. Try new varieties each season to see which ones work the best for you.

F, FF, or FFF means plants are resistant to fusarium wilt. VFN indicates that the plants are resistant to verticillium wilt, fusarium wilt, and root-knot nematodes; VFNT indicates resistance to these three diseases, plus tobacco mosaic virus. Plants resistant to tomato spotted wilt virus have TSWV on the plant tags.

Cherry and patio tomatoes are almost always a sure bet and are great for container gardens and small spaces. Some of my favorites are 'Jujube', an early and long-season producer of small, sweet as candy, crack-resistant fruits. Sweet 'Yellow Pear' is resistant to fusarium wilt, likes cooler weather, and adds good color to salsas. 'Black Mauri' is heirloom and a large cherry tomato with black hue as it ripens. It has a large tomato taste wrapped in a small tomato, making it good for roasting for roasted tomato pasta sauce. For eating fresh off the vine, slicing, and dicing, try 'Beaverlodge' series, ready to harvest in just 55 days and 'Glacier', also early, a sweet good slicer. 'Bonnie Best' is an old-time canning tomato, good for slicing too. 'Oregon Spring' can be planted early, takes light frost, and is ready in 75 days. 'Amish Paste', an heirloom, called the "ultimate paste tomato," and I agree, ready in 80 days. For greenhouse growing, try 'Cobra'. Its crack and disease resistance and smaller bushy growth makes it good for container gardens. Grafted tomatoes, plants that have been grafted onto a rootstock, much like fruit trees, improve disease resistance and vigor. Try 'Legend' (resistant to late blight), 'Yellow Pear', 'Oregon Spring', 'Cabernet', and 'Sweet Million'.

When and Where to Plant

Temperature: Tomatoes are absolute heat lovers. Transplant hardened-off, strong plants outdoors after all danger of frost. In cooler climes, provide some cover protection and try to keep the soil warm. When the plants are mature and setting fruit, they can take very light frosts with protection.

Soil: The soil should have compost that is well incorporated before planting or mix in slow-release, organic fertilizer such as Plant-tone.

Sun: Full sun.

How to Plant

Starting seeds indoors: Start seeds indoors eight to ten weeks before you want to plant tomatoes outdoors. Use a heat mat set to 70°F to 75°F and provide bright natural sunlight or use grow lights elevated 2 inches above the plants. After transplanting seedlings to pots, use a water-soluble, acid-loving fertilizer at ½ the rate once a week.

Planting outside: Harden off plants before planting them in the garden. Space plants 18 inches apart, and plant transplants 5 inches deep to encourage rooting from the stem and a deep root system.

For best results, keep tomatoes consistently and evenly watered.

How to Grow

Water: Tomatoes need steady, consistent moisture in order to avoid blossom-end rot (the end of the fruit opposite from the stem rots), a cultural problem that arises when calcium is deficient in the soil or watering is inconsistent. Use drip irrigation or soaker hoses to apply water slowly and directly at the roots, allowing the water to percolate deep into the soil.

GROWING TIPS

Place tomato cages and supports when you plant the plants while the plants are small and easy to tie. Poor or weak support systems make harvesting a tedious affair. Fruits lying on the ground are more susceptible to pests and rots.

Handpick tomato hornworms from dawn to dusk, when the fat green worms like to munch on the plants. Chipmunks and squirrels nibble at tomatoes if they're having a hard time finding water. There are organic repellents available to protect fruits. I have had good luck with interplanting taller bushier type marigolds and basil between the tomatoes. The critters are put off with their pungent aroma.

Yellow pear tomatoes are prolific producers.

Cracking fruit is caused by uneven irregular watering. Use drip irrigation or soaker hoses to avoid this problem.

Fertilizer: Avoid high-nitrogen fertilizer, which can cause more leaf growth than flower development. If soil tests and recommendations warrant it, apply potassium to improve flavor and disease resistance.

Pest control: Growing resistant varieties and keeping the plants healthy helps avoid many pest problems. Keep an eye out for tomato hornworms that feed on plants from dusk to early morning. Pick them off and squash them (or feed them to the chickens, who love them!).

Heat: You can turn up the heat for tomatoes. In cool summer areas, use black groundcover cloth to warm up soils; start with large, almost flowering or even in bud-state plants. Plan to provide crop protection cloth if temps drop in late summer or early autumn to protect fruit formation and ripening. In prolonged triple-digit summer temps, mulch the roots with straw to cool the soil down and provide some shade cloth in late afternoon. Plants can abort blooms in this type of situation. Most times I just try to wait the heat out when tomatoes will resume flowering and fruiting.

■ *When and How to Harvest*

Tomatoes are ripe when you need little effort to pull them off the plant. Leave tomatoes on the plant for as long as possible for the sweetest fruits.

WINTER SQUASH *(Cucurbita* spp.)

Winter squashes are planted in spring and into summer in Rocky Mountain regions, but the name is confusing because they still have to be harvested before frost. Winter squashes take a long time to grow and produce, but they can be stored over winter, hence the name. Large, fuzzy coated leaves are born on thick sprawling stems that hold funnel-shaped blooms, leading to massive plants that support the equally massive fruits through a long, hot growing season. They like the heat and use its warmth to build thick, tough skins and walls to protect the fruit within. These are all attributes that make the plant a bit drought tolerant. The fuzzy coating protects the leaves, the sprawling habit shades the roots, cooling the soil and holding in moisture. They have a deep-reaching root system too, which pulls moisture deep from within the soil. Use them in the edible landscape where you have that barren slope to cover as a double-duty exotic annual groundcover.

▓ *Recommended Varieties*

'Hunter' is the earliest butternut, ready in 85 days with a manageable small fruit averaging 2 pounds each with a long storage life. We like 'Carnival', an acorn squash that's pretty enough to take part in the fall floral centerpiece on our table and sweet enough to be the only acorn type we grow and store. Green, cream, yellow, and golden shells on a semidwarf vine make it a good container plant too. 'Small Wonder', harvested in 75 days, is a single serving-sized spaghetti squash. 'Small Sugar' pumpkins make wee jack-o-lanterns, and their bright orange, sugary sweet fruit is famous for its performance in pies. Each vine produces up to a half dozen sugar pumpkins. 'Orange Rave' makes dark orange, perfectly shaped, 15- to 25-pound fruits, perfect for carving and ready in about 100 days. For ornamental use, grow 'Jack be Little', cute mini-pumpkins maturing at just 3 to 4 inches across come in shades of orange and creamy white.

▓ *When and Where to Plant*

Temperature: Squashes need warm soil to grow. Plant outside when soil temperatures are at least 65°F.

Soil: Squashes grow well in our alkaline soils. Add compost to the soil before planting.

Sun: Full sun.

▓ *How to Plant*

Starting seeds indoors: In short growing seasons, start squash seeds four weeks before the last frost in peat or biodegradable pots to minimize shock at planting time.

Planting outside: Sow seeds or transplant hardened-off plants outside when soil temperatures are at least 65°F. Plant two to three seeds per hole or hill, 1 inch deep, 6 inches apart with hills 24 inches apart. When seedlings are 3 inches tall, use scissors to thin to two plants per hill.

How to Grow

Water: Keep squash deeply watered and apply straw mulch after the plants germinate or after planting.

Fertilizer: Sidedress with a balanced fertilizer every three weeks during the growing season.

Pest control: Squash bugs, squash vine borers, cucumber beetles, and Mexican bean beetles plague squash plants. Use row covers when plants are young to protect plants from the flying pests. You can raise the covers for two hours in the early morning a few days a week to allow insects to reach the flowers for pollination. Interplant with nasturtium and radishes to repel squash bugs. Allow the radish to go to seed to attract pollinators too.

Winter squash can be grown as an edible or as a decorative gourd.

When and How to Harvest

Winter squashes are ready to harvest when the skin has thickened and is dull, not shiny. Cut squashes from the vine, leaving 3 to 4 inches of stem. Wipe the soil off the fruits if no frost or rain threatens, leave them in the sun for a few days to harden off the rind for storage at 55°F to 70°F.

GROWING TIPS

Keep fruits from rotting while they grow by raising them up off the ground on planting flats or crates.

Mulch around the plants to keep the roots cool, keep the soil moist, and minimize weeds.

Winter squash plants are big and need a lot of room. If you have the inclination, you can build a sturdy trellis from pipe and wire and train them to climb. If you do this, you might need to support the fruits in homemade slings. Or plant them between corn or bean rows. They like the companionship!

Many herbs, such as sage, oregano, and thyme, are ornamental enough to be incorporated into flower gardens.

Warm-Season Herbs

Many of the herbs that flourish during warm weather are also cold hardy, but they don't grow and thrive during the cooler weather. For all of these herbs to produce fresh growth, ideal for cooking and preserving, they need full sun and warm temperatures.

Some warm-season herbs are perennials, while others are annuals. Perennial herbs are ideal for planting in pots, interplanted in the flower garden, edible landscape, or in a space all their own right outside your kitchen door. I have one large herb garden just out the backdoor. The sweeps of thyme, sage, oregano, and savory does double duty as part of the scented garden, interplanted with agastache, roses, and salvia. I also have my favorites and most-used herbs in pots that are moved into the greenhouse for winter, so I can have fresh cuts all winter long.

A note about planting times for these herbs: you can plant any and all of the warm-season herbs at the same time that you plant any warm-season vegetables. Hardy, perennial herbs can go outside earlier than tender annual herbs. The annual warm-season herbs usually need more water than the perennials, but many of the perennials listed here are drought-tolerant herbs as well.

Culantro is a good summer substitute for cilantro.

Cut off basil flowers to keep the plants producing fragrant, tender leaves.

BASIL *(Ocimum basilicum)*

During the summer growing season, rarely a salad, tomato, or pasta dish makes its way to the table without fresh basil being present. Dried basil still carries its sweetness in sauces and soups, and frozen into ice cubes in its peak of freshness, basil makes delicious pesto in the dead of winter. I try a new variety each season, collecting seeds from favored types to grow in subsequent years. Basil grows throughout the summer, and if it is clipped often, you can delay flowering until autumn. I grow a lot of it to eat, dry, and freeze, but also grow it for the great companion it makes with other crops, sweetening bell peppers and deterring rodents and pests with its heavenly scent when interplanted with tomatoes. Some contain more oil than others on tiny leaves that are quickly stripped from the stems and thrown into the dish without having to chop. Others are even prettier to look at, strutting their stuff with tiny red to purple flower spikes on branching bushy plants, making a lovely cut flower arrangement in the center of the table that smells divine.

GROWING TIPS

Cut the flowers off basil to encourage more production of fragrant leaves.

If basil plants get too leggy, just chop the plant back by two-thirds to one-half, water, and fertilize well.

Recommended Varieties

Some of my favored basil picks: 'Pestou' is a dense, mounding plant, maxing out at 12 inches tall. It is the chef's choice basil, high in oil (flavor) content and the leaves are tiny and easy to pull off the stems, no chopping required. 'Lemon' is basil with a twist. A hint of lemon makes it perfect for pesto, poultry, and fish, good in cocktails and lemonade too. Genovese 'Aroma 1' is classic pesto but shrubbier with smaller leaves, branching, and slow to flower. I use 'Christmas' basil, interplanted with peppers and tomatoes. Its 12- to 18-inch-tall bushy habit makes it a good barrier against ground-traveling pests. 'Christmas' has tall reddish-purple flower spikes that make long-lasting sweetly scented cut flowers, and its leaves are edible too. It comes back every year from self-sowing.

When and Where to Plant

Temperature: Plant outside when soil warms to at least 60°F.
Soil: Basil grows easily in most well-draining soils. Add compost to the soil before planting.
Sun: Full sun.

How to Plant

Starting seeds indoors: Start seeds indoors four weeks before planting outdoors.
Planting outside: Plant transplants outside, 12 inches apart.

How to Grow

Water: Basil isn't a heavy drinker, but keep it evenly moist.
Fertilizer: As with most herbs, basil doesn't require extra fertilizer.
Pest control: Japanese beetles and slugs are the most problematic pests for basil. There's not much you can do about Japanese beetles, but you can spread diatomaceous earth around the base of each plant to keep slugs from munching.

When and How to Harvest

Snip leaves from the top of the plant in the morning. Basil is a forgiving and fast-growing plant. You can chop off any piece of the plant, and it will regrow.

CHIVES *(Allium schoenoprasum)*

I brought a small clump of lemon chives in a plastic bag in the moving van when we moved to Utah. They are a hardy perennial, thriving, colonizing, and reseeding themselves in USDA Zones 4 and above. I wouldn't be at all surprised if they survived colder winters in the Rocky Mountain regions with a bit of straw protection. They are that tough. We use fresh clipped chives all season long. They are among the first perennials to pop up in early spring and the last to go dormant in early winter. Before they take their winter nap, I clip some bunches to dry and chop for the spice rack. Reconstituted, they have that just picked freshness. I added a drift of them to the meadow's edge and they have taken their place there, enjoying the full sun with other drought-tolerant trees, shrubs, grasses, and flowering bulbs for company.

Both the flowers and the stems of chives are edible.

■ *Recommended Varieties*

'Lemon' chives has a distinct lemony scent.

■ *When and Where to Plant*

Temperature: Plant chives outside in spring when soil temperatures are at least 60°F. Chives grow well in both cool springs and hot summers, as long as they have good water.

Soil: Chives are not picky about soil; they grow best in well-draining soils.

Sun: Full sun.

■ *How to Plant*

Starting seeds indoors: Start seeds indoors one month before planting outside.

Planting outside: Chives are easy to grow from seed. Sow seeds outdoors and cover with seed-starting mix. Keep seeds moist while germinating. Or plant divisions or starts from the nursery.

■ *How to Grow*

Water: Keep the soil evenly moist. Give extra water after cutting back.

Fertilizer: No extra fertilizer is needed.

Pest control: Chives have no pest problems.

■ *When and How to Harvest*

Keep chives producing leaves by cutting sections of the plant back to 3 inches tall once the whole plant is 6 to 8 inches tall. (Don't cut the entire plant back all the way to the ground.)

Chives are one of the earliest herbs to appear in the garden in spring.

GROWING TIPS

You can let chives flower, or you can cut the flowers off if you want the plants to keep producing leaves. The flowers are edible. If it is perennial in your area, divide to control the size of the clumps. Chives make good companions with carrots and are said to improve growth and flavor. They should not be planted with peas. They can deter aphids and munching pests if planted in the rose garden.

OREGANO *(Origanum* ssp.*)*

Oregano is versatile in the kitchen, easy to grow, and so pretty in the landscape and in containers, I cannot imagine my garden or table without it. It is a hardy creeping perennial (not as invasive as mint) that needs room to grow and not much else. It is one of the first herbs to send out new growth in early spring, and as soon as it reaches 6 inches tall, it is time for the first harvest. It makes for a great plant in the landscape on hills and slopes. Drought tolerant with its network of roots and natural air layering stems, oregano controls erosion. I planted a sweep of oregano in the herb garden, and it thrives in full sun and part shade as it meanders under the juniper and hackberry trees and tumbles over the rock wall. I use it so much in the kitchen that it shares a large container with an ornamental leucophyllum that overwinters in the greenhouse, so I have fresh oregano year-round.

■ Recommended Varieties

I have Greek oregano, which is hardy with a spicy flavor, and bears tiny white flowers. 'Hopley's Purple' has a mild oregano flavor and the added bonus of showy purplish red blooms. 'Amethyst Falls' is ornamental, cascading, with chartreuse and lavender hop-like blooms good in baskets.

■ When and Where to Plant

Temperature: Plant oregano outside after danger of frost has passed.
Soil: Oregano grows best in our alkaline, well-drained soils.
Sun: Full sun.

■ How to Plant

Starting seeds indoors: You can start seeds of unique varieties indoors. Sprinkle them on the soil surface, cover lightly with sand, and keep the seeds moist as the plantsgerminate.
Planting outside: Plant starts outdoors as soon as the ground is workable.

Oregano is often known as the "pizza" herb.

Growing oregano in a pot ensures it won't hog all of the space in your vegetable garden.

■ *How to Grow*

Water: No extra water is needed after plants have established themselves, except in periods of summer drought. Water deeply.

Fertilizer: No extra fertilizer is needed.

Pest control: Aphids and spider mites can attack oregano when it's very dry outside. Water the plant if your region is experiencing drought. The insects will eventually go away. It's almost impossible to kill oregano.

■ *When and How to Harvest*

Leaves are most fragrant just before the flowers open, but you can snip leaves off to use at any time. To harvest for drying, cut stems during first flush of spring growth when they are 6 to 8 inches tall, cutting the plant back to 3 inches. Put entire stems on drying racks or in paper bags with a few air holes to dry. Store stems with leaves intact to retain oils. Pull off leaves as you need them.

GROWING TIP

Give oregano room to grow. Even though it is a clumping perennial herb, the stems will form roots and spread if allowed to. Cut the plant back all the way to the new flush of green growth in spring. Dig and divide to control size or install edging to discourage creeping growth.

ROSEMARY *(Rosmarinus officinalis)*

We grew rosemary in southern California's Mediterranean climate as a landscape plant. It was used to control erosion on slopes, to fill tight spaces in median strips, and as a drought-tolerant groundcover and shrub. The fact that you could eat it was just a bonus. Here in USDA Zone 5, it requires a bit more attention. I have a couple of pots of rosemary that come out of the greenhouse before the last frost to bask in the late winter sun. In the heat of the summer, when the pots heat up and the soil with them, I move the pots to the shade. They are not as inclined to flower there and more intent on putting out new foliage, which is the part I use in the kitchen. I use it mostly fres, but also dry some long stems so I have some in the spice rack when dried rosemary is called for.

Recommended Varieties

'Arp' is the most cold hardy, growing in USDA Zone 5 winters with protection. Prostrate types are good in hanging baskets and containers. 'Barbeque' has long branches food for kebobs, growing to 4 to 5 feet tall, good for larger containers.

When and Where to Plant

Temperature: Plant transplants outside after danger of frost has passed for best establishment.

Soil: Rosemary is widely adaptable to many different soil types but must have excellent drainage.

Sun: Full sun.

How to Plant

Starting seeds indoors: Not recommended.

Planting outside: Grow rosemary from transplants. Plant transplants outside where they'll have room to grow to be at least 3 feet wide and 3 feet tall over time.

GROWING TIPS

Once rosemary is established, don't water it unless your area is experiencing a severe drought. Don't feed, as that promotes weak growth that's susceptible to pests. Rosemary is extremely rabbit and deer resistant.

■ *When and How to Grow*

Water: No extra water is needed once plants are established except during long periods of summer drought. Check the soil with your finger, and if it is dry down to 2 inches, then apply water slowly and deeply.

Fertilizer: No extra fertilizer is needed.

Pest control: Spider mites can occasionally afflict rosemary. Use horticultural oil to treat the plant for these pests.

■ *When and How to Harvest*

Cut pieces of rosemary at any time of the year to use for cooking. The young tips are best for mixing into fresh salads. The rest of the plant is good for use in soups, stews, or roasting.

Use straight branches of rosemary as shish kabob sticks.

SAGE *(Salvia officinalis)*

Culinary sage plays an important edible landscape role as the star of my herb garden. I planted the starts from 2-inch pots spaced 8 inches apart six years ago. Each spring, it starts sending out new tufts of aromatic oval green on top, lighter green to almost white on the bottom, softy fuzzy leaves. As soon as the green growth is 4 inches tall, we do the only maintenance required for the year, by going after the top older woody stems with a string trimmer. Within a few weeks, the plants are mounding, thick, and beautiful, sweeping in a large drift, partially shaded by junipers and wisteria and creeping into the full sun where it shares space with the catmint. It sends out lavender to purple flower spikes, but there are ample leaves on the stems for use in the kitchen, so I let it do what it wants to do naturally. Sage is a hardy perennial in USDA Zones 5 and higher, very drought tolerant, and even when snow is falling, it retains some foliage under the protection of the juniper, so I can dash out at Thanksgiving to grab a few fresh leaves for the stuffing.

■ *Recommended Varieties*

Beyond the straight species of garden sage, there are many varieties with interesting colors of leaves, increased cold hardiness, and other desirable characteristics. 'Berggarten' sage is a hardier, more compact variety than the straight species of sage. 'Purpurascens' is also a garden sage that has deep purple leaves. 'Tricolor' sage has leaves that are purple, green, and white. It is decorative and useful. 'Icterina' sage has variegated green and yellow leaves as does 'Aurea'. The variegated types are not as hardy but are great in containers.

GROWING TIPS

For more fragrant leaves, cut off sage flowers when they appear. The plant will channel more of its energy into leaf production, which is the part you cook with anyway.

Replant garden sage every three to four years for fresh, new growth, taking cuttings off existing plants for replanting. If the plant is hardy in your area, cut back hard each spring, so that it will retain its soft fresh new growth habit. When you cut it back, that's a good time to check to see if any plants are not coming out of dormancy. Those can be replaced at that time.

Sage makes a great potted plant. Bring it indoors and place in a sunny window for winter growing.

■ *When and Where to Plant*

Temperature: Garden sage is at its best and highest oil content in the summer.

Soil: Plant in well-drained soil.

Sun: Garden sage needs full sun to be most productive and for leaves to be the most fragrant. In hottest summer regions, some afternoon shade is best.

Sage grows best from cuttings.

■ *How to Plant*

Starting seeds indoors: Grow sage from cuttings or buy starts. To take cuttings, use pruners to cut off the top 4 inches of tender new growth. Strip off leaves from the lower half and stick it in potting soil. Once the plant has established good roots (you can pull up on the plant without uprooting it), transplant it outside.

Planting outside: Plant outside when all danger of frost has passed, spacing plants 8 inches apart for mass plantings or 12 inches apart for single plants.

■ *How to Grow*

Water: Once established, sage needs no extra water. Water only during hot summers with no monsoonal rains. Watch the plants for signs of wilting, check the soil to be sure it is dry down about 2 inches, then water slowly and deeply.

Fertilizer: Sage does not usually need extra fertilizer.

Pest control: Slugs may attack sage when conditions are wetter than usual, and spider mites can be a problem during times of extreme drought. Both problems will go away on their own, eventually.

■ *When and How to Harvest*

Cut stems or individual leaves to use when cooking. To harvest for drying, cut at midday when oil content is the highest. Cut stems 4 to 6 inches long, bundle two or three together, tie and hang in a dry location until dry. Store stems with leaves intact in a large airtight container; grind leaves to use.

SAVORY Winter and Summer *(Satureja montana, S. hortensis)*

The first time I smelled savory, I had delicious memories of thyme, mint, and oregano, all mixed into one. I instantly purchased the diminutive starts. One was a summer savory, looking very much like its relative, the hardy, winter savory. I planted them both, side by side at the front of the herb border, where I could do my own taste trials and so that I could see how they fared in the landscape. The summer savory is the strongest in flavor and best used fresh, snipped just as the plant starts to bud, as that is when the oil content is the highest. The summer savory didn't put on as much growth as the winter variety, and it seemed to have a more difficult time dealing with watering conditions prevalent in the low-water-use herb bed. The winter savory, hardy to Zones 5 and up, has a milder, yet still distinctive savory flavor that holds the oils in the dried product. I use it fresh sprinkled on fish and poultry and sprinkle it dried in soups, stews, and sauces. It is versatile in the kitchen and durable in the edible landscape as a foreground border plant or groundcover.

Loved by pollinators, the winter savory is beginning to bloom.

■ Recommended Varieties

Purchase winter or summer savory in pots from your local garden center.

■ When and Where to Plant

Temperature: Savory grows best in warm temperatures. Plant transplants or starts outside after all danger of frost has passed for best results.

Soil: Savory needs well-drained soil to grow.

Sun: Full sun.

■ How to Plant

Starting seeds indoors: Not recommended.

Planting outside: It is much easier to grow savory from starts. Try to find a local herb grower for the best product that has been grown in your area. If the herbs are bought in from out of your state, then be sure to harden them off in the area you will plant before putting them in the ground.

■ How to Grow

Water: Savory needs deep but infrequent watering. Allow the soil to dry out between waterings.

Fertilizer: Savory needs no additional fertilizer.

Pest control: No pests that I know of.

■ When and How to Harvest

If it is growing in the ground, harvest just as soon as you can grab it by the handful at the first flush of spring growth to dry and store or clip it for fresh use anytime. The flowers are edible too.

GROWING TIP

If you have heavy clay soil that drains poorly or live in a colder climate zone, grow savory in a pot.

Fresh or dried, thyme makes a great flavoring for meats or vinegars.

THYME *(Thymus vulgaris)*

I have a sizable bed in the herb garden that is devoted to thyme. Grown as a hardy perennial in Zones 4 and above, the plot makes quick work of the main harvest at the beginning of spring. Tiny aromatic leaves come out in tufts as soon as the snow melts. The stems are twiggy, becoming more woody as they mature, making them unchewable, necessitating removing the tiny leaves before using. The plants flourish in the sun and in the raising temps, so I harvest the new growth as soon as I can grab handfuls to give the bed a "crew cut," using the new softer growth for drying and storing for winter use. When it fills back in, it begins to set flower, tiny white blooms that serve as bee magnets. Creeping thyme fills in spaces between pavers and steps, their scent filling the air with my trodding. Hardy, drought tolerant, and thriving in our alkaline soils, thyme is front and center in the herb garden, the edible, low-water-use landscape, in containers and baskets, and—in my kitchen!

■ *Recommended Varieties*

There are many varieties, sizes, and forms of thyme, including flavored, variegated, upright, clumping, and minicreeping. Try caraway-scented, lemon, lime, or orange balsam for flavor-infused thyme. Creeping thyme types that are cold hardy to Zone 4 are Pink Creeping, 'Reiter', 'Ohme Garden Carpet', and 'Red Mother of Thyme'. Variegated thyme is good for containers.

GROWING TIPS

If you have heavy clay soil that drains poorly, grow thyme in a pot. Plant thyme in the garden along with other vegetables to help repel pests.

When and Where to Plant

Temperature: Thyme grows best in warm temperatures. Plant thyme plants outside after all danger of frost has passed for best results.

Soil: Thyme needs well-drained soil to grow. It will rot if kept wet.

Sun: Full sun.

How to Plant

Starting seeds indoors: Not recommended.

Planting outside: Grow thyme from cuttings. Root cuttings by snipping off 4-inch pieces of fresh, green growth from a plant. Strip the leaves off the lower half and place it in a cup of water. Once the plant has developed roots, plant it in a 4-inch pot. When the plant has rooted in, transplant it outside. Also purchase plants at your local garden center or online.

How to Grow

Water: Thyme does not need extra water once established.

Fertilizer: Fertilize once a year in spring with a balanced, slow-release fertilizer.

Pest control: Spider mites will attack the plant if it is stressed—usually during drought. Fungal diseases and root rot are also problems if the soil is wet.

When and How to Harvest

Thyme leaves are most fragrant if they are cut before the plant flowers. Keep cutting back the top 4 to 6 inches of growth to stimulate fresh, new growth, which is best for cooking.

Harvest thyme before the flowers appear.

RESOURCES

This list is not comprehensive, but it includes resources I use for inspiration, information, and advice.

Books

Rocky Mountain Gardener's Guide, John Cretti, Cool Springs Press, 2003
Month-by-Month Gardening in the Rocky Mountains, John Cretti, Cool Springs Press, 2005
All New Square-Foot Gardening, Mel Bartholomew, Cool Springs Press, 2005
Straw Bale Gardens, Joel Karsten, Cool Springs Press, 2013
The Heirloom Life Gardener, Jere & Emilee Gettle, Hyperion Press, 2011
Carrots Love Tomatoes, Louise Riotte, Storey Publishing, 1998
Growing Fruit & Vegetables, Richard Bird, Hermes House, 2003
Edible Landscaping, Second Edition, Rosalind Creasy, Sierra Club Books, 2010
The Edible Front Yard, Ivette Soler, Timber Press, 2011

Magazines

Heirloom Gardener, 2278 Baker Creek Road, Mansfield, MO 65704,
    www.heirloomgardener.com
Horticulture, P.O. Box 420235, Palm Coast, FL 32142, www.hortmag.com
Organic Gardening, 400 South Tenth Street, Emmaus, PA 18098,
    www.organicgardening.com

Resources

Cooperative Extension: offers soil testing, tissue testing for disease, educational programs, Master Gardener training, brochures, pamphlets, videos, and other informational publications related to home gardening, fruit, vegetable, herb growing, bee keeping, composting, soil management, pest control, and much more. Visit www.csrees.usda.gov to find the closest Cooperative Extension office in your area.

Colleges

State universities, colleges, and community colleges offer coursework devoted to horticulture sciences. Many offer free classes, community education opportunities, demonstration gardens, student-run nurseries and plant sales, and other public gardening events.

Colorado: Colorado State University, www.hortla.agsci.colostate.edu
       Front Range Community College, www.frontrange.edu
Idaho: College of Western Idaho, www.cwidaho.cc/academics/horticulture
       College of Southern Idaho, www.agriculture.csl.edu/horticulture/
Montana: Montana State University, www.plantsciences.montana.edu

Utah: Utah State University, www.psc.usu.edu/htm/undergraduate/
ornamental-horticulture/
Wyoming: Northern Wyoming Community College District, Sheridan College,
www.sheridan.edu
Western Wyoming Community College, www.wwcc.wy.edu

Websites

Dave's Garden
www.davesgarden.com

Hunter
www.hunterindustries.com/
homeowners

Master Composter
wwwmastercomposter.com

Mother Earth News
www.motherearthnews.com

Old Farmers Almanac
www.almanac.com/content/vegetable-
garden-planner

Plants, Seeds, Gardening Supplies

Baker Creek Heirloom Seeds
2278 Baker Creek Road
Mansfield, MO 65704
www.rareseeds.com

Renee's Garden
6060 Graham Hill Rd.
Felton, CA 95018
www.reneesgarden.com

Johnny's Selected Seeds
955 Benton Avenue
Winslow, ME 04901
www.Johnnyseeds.com

Seeds of Change
P.O. Box 152
Spicer, MN 56288
www.seedsofchange.com

The Natural Gardening Company
P.O. Box 750776
Petaluma, CA 94975
www.naturalgardening.com

Growers Supply
1440 Field of Dreams Way
Dyersville, IA 52040
www.GrowersSupply.com

Netafim USA
5470 East Home Ave.
Fresno, CA 93727
www.netafimusa.com

Rain Bird Irrigation
970 West Sierra Madre Ave.
Azusa, CA 91702
www.rainbird.com/homeowner/
products/drip/

GLOSSARY

Acidic soil: On a soil pH scale of 0 to 14, acidic soil has a pH lower than 5.5. Most garden plants prefer a soil a bit on the acidic side.

Afternoon sun: A garden receiving afternoon sun typically has full sun from 1:00 p.m. to 5:00 p.m. daily, with more shade during the morning hours.

Alkaline soil: On a soil pH scale of 0 to 14, alkaline soil has a pH higher than 7.0. Many desert plants thrive in slightly alkaline soils.

Annual: A plant that germinates (sprouts), flowers, and dies within one year or season (spring, summer, winter, or fall) is an annual.

***Bacillus thuringiensis* (B.t.):** *B.t.* is an organic pest control based on naturally occurring soil bacteria, often used to control harmful caterpillars such as cutworms, leaf rollers, and webworms.

Balled and burlapped (B&B): This phrase describes plants that have been grown in field nursery rows, dug up with their soil intact, wrapped with burlap, and tied with twine. Most of the plants sold balled and burlapped are large evergreen plants and deciduous trees.

Bare root: Bare-root plants are those that are shipped dormant, without being planted in soil or having soil around their roots. Roses are often shipped bare root.

Beneficial insects: These insects perform valuable services such as pollination and pest control. Ladybugs, soldier beetles, and some bees are examples.

Biennial: A plant that blooms during its second year and then dies is a biennial.

Bolting: This is a process when a plant switches from leaf growth to producing flowers and seeds. Bolting often occurs quite suddenly and is usually undesirable, because the plant usually dies shortly after bolting.

Brown materials: A part of a well-balanced compost pile, brown materials include high-carbon materials such as brown leaves and grass, woody plant stems, dryer lint, and sawdust.

Bud: The bud is an undeveloped shoot nestled between the leaf and the stem that will eventually produce a flower or plant branch.

Bush: *See* shrub.

Cane: A stem on a fruit shrub; usually blackberry or raspberry stems are called canes, but blueberry stems can also be referred to as canes.

Central leader: The term for the center trunk of a fruit tree.

Chilling hours: Hours when the air temperature is below 45°F; chilling hours are related to fruit production.

Common name: A name that is generally used to identify a plant in a particular region, as opposed to its botanical name, which is standard throughout the world; for example, the common name for *Echinacea purpurea* is "purple coneflower."

Contact herbicide: This type of herbicide kills only the part of the plant that it touches, such as the leaves or the stems.

Container: Any pot or vessel that is used for planting; containers can be ceramic, clay, steel, or plastic—or a teacup, bucket, or barrel.

Container grown: This describes a plant that is grown, sold, and shipped while in a pot.

Cool-season annual: This is a flowering plant, such as snapdragon or pansy, that thrives during cooler months.

Cool-season vegetable: This is a vegetable, such as spinach, broccoli, and peas, that thrives during cooler months.

Cover crop: These plants are grown specifically to enrich the soil, prevent erosion, suppress weeds, and control pests and diseases.

Cross-pollinate: This describes the transfer of pollen from one plant to another plant.

Dappled shade: This is bright shade created by high tree branches or tree foliage, where patches of sunlight and shade intermingle.

Day-neutral plant: A plant that flowers when it reaches a certain size, regardless of the day length, is a day-neutral plant.

Deadhead: To remove dead flowers in order to encourage further bloom and prevent the plant from going to seed is to deadhead.

Deciduous plant: A plant that loses its leaves seasonally, typically in fall or early winter, is deciduous.

Diatomaceous earth: A natural control for snails, slugs, flea beetles, and other garden pests, diatomaceous earth consists of ground-up fossilized remains of sea creatures.

Dormancy: The period when plants stop growing in order to conserve energy, this happens naturally and seasonally, usually in winter.

Drip line: The ground area under the outer circumference of tree branches, this is where most of the tree's roots that absorb water and nutrients are found.

Dwarf: In the context of fruit gardening, a dwarf fruit tree is a tree that grows no taller than 10 feet tall and is usually a dwarf as a result of the rootstock of the tree.

Evergreen: A plant that keeps its leaves year-round, instead of dropping them seasonally, is evergreen.

Floating row covers: Lightweight fabric that can be used to protect plants from pests. Usually white in color.

Floricane: A second-year cane on a blackberry or raspberry shrub; floricanes are fruit bearing.

Flower stalk: The stem that supports the flower and elevates it so that insects can reach the flower and pollinate it is the flower stalk.

Frost: Ice crystals that form when the temperature falls below freezing (32°F) create frost.

Full sun: Areas of the garden that receive direct sunlight for six to eight hours a day or more, with no shade, are in full sun.

Fungicide: This describes a chemical compound used to control fungal diseases.

Gallon container: A standard nursery-sized container for plants, a gallon container is roughly equivalent to a gallon container of milk.

Garden fork: A garden implement with a long handle and short tines; use a garden fork for loosening and turning soil.

Garden lime: This soil amendment lowers soil acidity and raises the pH.

Garden soil: The existing soil in a garden bed; it is generally evaluated by its nutrient content and texture. Garden soil is also sold as a bagged item at garden centers and home-improvement stores.

Germination: This is the process by which a plant emerges from a seed or a spore.

Grafted tree: This is a tree composed of two parts: the top, or scion, which bears fruit, and the bottom, or rootstock.

Graft union: This is the place on a fruit tree trunk where the rootstock and the scion have been joined.

Granular fertilizer: This type of fertilizer comes in a dry, pellet-like form rather than a liquid or powder.

Green materials: An essential element in composting that includes grass clippings, kitchen scraps, and manure and provides valuable nitrogen in the pile.

Hand pruners: An important hand tool that consists of two sharp blades that perform a scissoring motion, these are used for light pruning, clipping, and cutting.

Hardening off: This is the process of slowly acclimating seedlings and young plants grown in an indoor environment to the outdoors.

Hardiness zone map: This map lists average annual minimum temperature ranges of a particular area. This information is helpful in determining appropriate plants for the garden. North America is divided into eleven separate hardiness zones.

Hard rake: This tool has a long handle and rigid tines at the bottom. It is great for moving a variety of garden debris, such as soil, mulch, leaves, and pebbles.

Heirloom: A plant that was more commonly grown pre-World War II.

Hoe: A long-handled garden tool with a short, narrow, flat steel blade, it is used for breaking up hard soil and removing weeds.

Hose breaker: This device screws onto the end of a garden hose to disperse the flow of water from the hose.

Hybrid: Plants produced by crossing two genetically different plants, hybrids often have desirable characteristics such as disease resistance.

Insecticide: This substance is used for destroying or controlling insects that are harmful to plants. Insecticides are available in organic and synthetic forms.

Irrigation: A system of watering the landscape, irrigation can be an in-ground automatic system, soaker or drip hoses, or hand-held hoses with nozzles.

Jute twine: A natural-fiber twine, jute is used for gently staking plants or tying them to plant supports.

Larva: The immature stage of an insect that goes through complete metamorphosis; caterpillars are butterfly or moth larvae.

Larvae: This is the plural of larva.

Liquid fertilizer: Plant fertilizer in a liquid form; some types need to be mixed with water, and some types are ready to use from the bottle.

Long-day plant: Plants that flower when the days are longer than their critical photoperiod. Long-day plants typically flower in early summer, when the days are still getting longer.

Loppers: One of the largest manual gardening tools, use loppers for pruning branches of 1 to 3 inches in diameter with a scissoring motion.

Morning sun: Areas of the garden that have an eastern exposure and receive direct sun in the morning hours are in morning sun.

Mulch: Any type of material that is spread over the soil surface around the base of plants to suppress weeds and retain soil moisture is mulch.

Nematode: Microscopic, wormlike organisms that live in the soil; some nematodes are beneficial, while others are harmful.

New wood (new growth): The new growth on plants, it is characterized by a greener, more tender form than older, woodier growth.

Nozzle: A device that attaches to the end of a hose and disperses water through a number of small holes; the resulting spray covers a wider area.

Old wood: Old wood is growth that is more than one year old. Some fruit plants produce on old wood. If you prune these plants in spring before they flower and fruit, you will cut off the wood that will produce fruit.

Organic: This term describes products derived from naturally occurring materials instead of materials synthesized in a lab.

Part shade: Areas of the garden that receive three to six hours of sun a day are in part shade. Plants requiring part shade will often require protection from the more intense afternoon sun, either from tree leaves or from a building.

Part sun: Areas of the garden that receive three to six hours of sun a day are in part sun. Although the term is often used interchangeably with "part shade," a "part sun" designation places greater emphasis on the minimal sun requirements.

Perennial: A plant that lives for more than two years is a perennial. Examples include trees, shrubs, and some flowering plants.

pH: A figure designating the acidity or the alkalinity of garden soil, pH is measured on a scale of 1 to 14, with 7.0 being neutral.

Pinch: This is a method to remove unwanted plant growth with your fingers, promoting bushier growth and increased blooming.

Pitchfork: A hand tool with a long handle and sharp metal prongs, a pitchfork is typically used for moving loose material such as mulch or hay.

Plant label: This label or sticker on a plant container provides a description of the plant and information on its care and growth habits.

Pollination: The transfer of pollen for fertilization from the male pollen-bearing structure (stamen) to the female structure (pistil), usually by wind, bees, butterflies, moths, or hummingbirds; this process is required for fruit production.

Potting soil: A mixture used to grow flowers, herbs, and vegetables in containers, potting soil provides proper drainage and extra nutrients for healthy growth.

Powdery mildew: A fungal disease characterized by white powdery spots on plant leaves and stems, this is worse during times of drought or when plants have poor air circulation.

Pre-emergent herbicide: This weedkiller works by preventing weed seeds from sprouting.

Primocane: A first-year cane on a blackberry shrub, a primocane doesn't produce fruit.

Pruning: This is a garden task in which a variety of hand tools are used to remove dead or overgrown branches to increase plant fullness and health.

Pruning saw: This hand tool for pruning smaller branches and limbs features a long, serrated blade with an elongated handle.

Rhizome: An underground horizontal stem that grows side shoots, a rhizome is similar to a bulb.

Rootball: The network of roots and soil clinging to a plant when it is lifted out of the ground is the rootball.

Rootstock: The bottom part of a grafted fruit tree, rootstocks are often used to create dwarf fruit trees, impart pest or disease resistance, or make a plant more cold hardy.

Runner: A stem sprouting from the center of a strawberry plant, a runner produces fruit in its second year.

Scaffold branch: This horizontal branch emerges almost perpendicular to the trunk.

Scientific name: This two-word identification system consists of the genus and species of a plant, such as *Ilex opaca*.

Scion: The top, fruit-bearing part of a grafted fruit tree is the scion.

Scissors: A two-bladed hand tool great for cutting cloth, paper, twine, and other lightweight materials, scissors are a basic garden tool.

Seed packet: The package in which vegetable and flower seeds are sold, it typically includes growing instructions, a planting chart, and harvesting information.

Seed-starting mix: Typically a soil-less blend of perlite, vermiculite, peat moss, and other ingredients, seed-starting mix is specifically formulated for growing plants from seed.

Self-fertile: A plant that does not require cross-pollination from another plant in order to produce fruit is self-fertile.

Semidwarf: A fruit tree grafted onto a rootstock that restricts growth of the tree to one-half to two-thirds of its natural size is semidwarf.

Shade: Garden shade is the absence of any direct sunlight in a given area, usually due to tree foliage or building shadows.

Short-day plant: Flowering when the length of day is shorter than its critical photoperiod, short-day plants typically bloom during fall, winter, or early spring.

Shredded hardwood mulch: A mulch consisting of shredded wood that interlocks, resisting washout and suppressing weeds.

Shrub: This woody plant is distinguished from a tree by its multiple trunks and branches and its shorter height of less than 15 feet tall.

Sidedress: To sprinkle slow-release fertilizer along the side of a plant row or plant stem is to sidedress.

Slow-release fertilizer: This form of fertilizer releases nutrients at a slower rate throughout the season, requiring less-frequent applications.

Snips: This hand tool, used for snipping small plants and flowers, is perfect for harvesting fruits, vegetables, and flowers.

Soaker hose: This is an efficient watering system in which a porous hose, usually made from recycled rubber, allows water to seep out around plant roots.

Soil knife: This garden knife with a sharp, serrated edge is used for cutting twine, plant roots, turf, and other garden materials.

Soil test: An analysis of a soil sample, this determines the level of nutrients (to identify deficiencies) and detects pH.

Spur: This is a small, compressed, fruit-bearing branch on a fruit tree.

Standard: Describing a fruit tree grown on its own seedling rootstock or a nondwarfing rootstock, this is the largest of the three sizes of fruit trees.

Sucker: The odd growth from the base of a tree or a woody plant, often caused by stress, this also refers to sprouts from below the graft of a rose or fruit tree. Suckers divert energy away from the desirable tree growth and should be removed.

Systemic herbicide: This type of weedkiller is absorbed by the plant's roots and taken into the roots to destroy all parts of the plant.

Taproot: This is an enlarged, tapered plant root that grows vertically downward.

Thinning: This is the practice of removing excess vegetables (root crops) to leave more room for the remaining vegetables to grow; also refers to the practice of removing fruits when still small from fruit trees so that the remaining fruits can grow larger.

Topdress: To spread fertilizer on top of the soil (usually around fruit trees or vegetables) is to topdress.

Transplants: Plants that are grown in one location and then moved to and replanted in another; seeds started indoors and nursery plants are two examples.

Tree: This woody perennial plant typically consists of a single trunk with multiple lateral branches.

Tree canopy: This is the upper layer of growth, consisting of the tree's branches and leaves.

Tropical plant: This is a plant that is native to a tropical region of the world, and thus acclimated to a warm, humid climate and not hardy to frost.

Warm-season vegetable: This is a vegetable that thrives during the warmer months. Examples are tomatoes, okra, and peppers. These vegetables do not tolerate frost.

Watering wand: This hose attachment features a longer handle for watering plants beyond reach.

Water sprout: This vertical shoot emerges from a scaffold branch. It is usually nonfruiting and undesirable.

NOTES

INDEX

PHOTO CREDITS

Tom Eltzroth: pp. 70, 72, 81, 185

Katie Elzer-Peters: pp. 11, 19, 20, 23, 24, 26, 27, 28 (all), 31, 33, 35, 36, 37, 42, 44, 45, 46, 47, 48 (both), 50, 52, 55, 66 (all), 73, 122, 127, 128, 130, 132, 138, 142, 144, 148, 152, 156, 157, 158, 159, 160, 162, 163, 165, 167, 173, 176, 178, 179, 182, 190, 191, 192, 195, 196, 205, 208, 209

iStock: pp. 22, 53, 56, 60, 63 (bottom), 74, 75, 83, 84, 85, 99, 106, 118, 140, 150, 153, 177, 186, 199, 201

Jupiter Images: pp. 80

Diana Maranhao: pp. 77, 102, 206

Shutterstock: pp. 9, 41, 61, 78, 88, 90, 91, 97, 98, 121, 134, 137, 147, 168, 170, 174, 181, 189, 203

Photo courtesy of Stark Bro's., www.starkbros.com: pp. 68, 69

Lynn Steiner: pp. 6, 154, 194, 198, 200

Superstock: pp. 58

Thinkstock: pp. 108

MEET DIANA MARANHAO

Diana (Dee) Maranhao has been an active member of the horticulture/landscape industry for over 35 years. The majority of her professional career was spent in higher education, serving as horticulture program manager, nursery production specialist, and as an educator specializing in xeriscape-low water use landscaping, greenhouse nursery management, and plant propagation. She developed the program *Xeriscape for the Classroom* and presented the monthly workshop to K–12 educators to bring water conservation gardening techniques to children in the classroom. The course syllabus is still being presented today. Diana developed and taught a full-day, intensive, hands-on workshop for educators on "Building School Gardens," which addressed designing school gardens, grant search, and educational program development.

Upon retiring from her long tenure in education, Diana has served as horticulture editor and project editor for numerous educational texts, magazines, garden guides, and horticulture book titles. She has been a regular featured garden columnist for more than ten years, authoring hundreds of gardening and horticulture articles for the public and for the horticulture industry. Combining her professional background and education with the constant learning experience her home gardens provide, she serves to encourage, to teach, and to inspire others to garden, and to do so with water conservation and sustainability of natural resources in mind.

Diana has an associate in science degree in ornamental horticulture from Cuyamaca College in San Diego, completion certificates in copyediting from the University of California, and merchandising from Kinman Business University, and holds a life-time teaching credential in California specializing in ornamental horticulture. She is currently the administrative assistant for the Desert Green Foundation, Las Vegas, a nonprofit group that presents a yearly educational conference for professionals to encourage continued learning in the landscape industry.

Diana and her husband, Steve, live and garden in southern Utah. Since moving to their little plot of land, they have planted over 100 low-water-use trees, shrubs, and perennials, intermingled with vineyard, orchard, vegetable, herb, and flower gardens.